Turn On Tune In
Drop Out

Timothy Leary

RONIN

Turn On, Tune In, Drop Out
ISBN: 978-1-57951-009-1
Copyright 1965, 1966, 1967, 1968, 1990, 1999 by Timothy Leary

Published by
RONIN Publishing, Inc.
PO Box 22900
Oakland Ca 94609
www.roninpub.com

Project Editor:	Beverly A. Potter, PhD	*docpotter.com*
Cover Design:	Brian Groppe	*Brian Groppe.com*
Paste Up:	Regent Press	*regentpress.net*

Library of Congress Card Number: 2009922666
Printed in the United States of America
Distributed to the book trade by PGW/Perseus

Previously published as *Politics of Ecstasy*, chapters 12-22

Foreword

Hermes was the messenger of the gods and the brother of the goddess of wisdom, Athena. He was also something of a trickster. And, in his incarnation as Hermes Trismagistus, he served the role of being an initiator into the mystical depths of the ancient wisdom schools. Thus esoteric knowledge was once known as Hermeticism. Zeus rather liked him and made him his naughty messenger.

Like Hermes, Timothy Leary was an "avowed rascal"—and his very delightful and poetic writings on the subject (he had an almost unparalled gift for word play), indicate that he understood the role of the rascal in an elevated, cosmological sense—i.e., the archetype of the trickster.

The old panthiestic religions understood the importance of the trickster as a figure for spiritual awakening. So did the shamanistic cultures. Trickster is a major figure in American Indian folk wisdom. And also in Sufi tales. Leary implied that there is a certain type of "rascal"—with a certain grin and wink (and wisdom beyond wisdom)—who, in a spiritual sense, were far more trustworthy than the more sober types.

In the Zen tradition, this is known as the School of Crazy Wisdom. Leary, himself, studied, or was otherwise acquainted with the masters of this tradition—Aleister Crowley, Milarepa, Ken Kesey, Lao Tsu, and Alan Ginsberg to name a few. But, Timothy

Leary—in his own inimitable way—has become the twentieth century's grand master of crazy wisdom, the Hermes of our age.

In 1966, when I first heard the mantra, "Tune In, Turn On, Drop Out," I was a well-adjusted college student in Wisconsin—planning to major in business administration. I expected to live a life according to the pattern that I saw established for me—help out in my father's furniture and real-estate businesses and probably take them over, drink beer on the weekends and milk during the week. I had no inkling then that I was destined for a career communicating the realities of intuition, parapsychology and the wisdom traditions to the millions via television, radio and the internet. But, as I look back now on my own spiritual awakening, I can say that I responded—as did millions of my baby-boomer compatriots—to the siren call of Timothy Leary beckoning us to see reality in a fresher and larger way.

I admire Leary's work as a pioneer, a visionary, an explorer of consciousness, a systematizer, a social revolutionary and a scientist. But, I also realize that if Timothy Leary's life were to be examined from the perspective of conventional morality, we would see a very different story. And the list of his high crimes and misdemeanors would be long indeed. So to me, Timothy Leary's life and work stands as a testament to the value of crazy wisdom, to the Hermetic trickster archetype—in spite of the fact that this archetype will almost always encounter disapproval from the guardians of conventional morality and the status quo

—Jeffrey Mishlove, Ph.D.
Host, *Thinking Allowed*
(National Public Television series)
Author, *The Roots of Consciousness*
President, Intuition Network

Table Of Contents

You are God: Remember!

Cover of the first privately printed edition of
Start Your Own Religion (1967).

1

Start Your Own Religion

The Purpose of Life Is Religious Discovery

That intermediate manifestation of the divine process which we call the DNA code has spent the last 2 billion years making this planet a Garden of Eden. An intricate web has been woven, a delicate fabric of chemical-electrical-seed-tissue-organism-species. A dancing, joyous harmony of energy transactions is rooted in the 12 inches of topsoil which covers the rock

metal

fire

core of this planet.

Into this Garden of Eden each human being is born perfect. We were all born divine mutants, the DNA code's best answer to joyful survival on this planet. An exquisite package for adaptation based on 2 billion years of consumer research (RNA) and product design (DNA).

But each baby, although born perfect, immediately finds himself in an imperfect, artificial, disharmonious social system which systematically robs him of his divinity.

And the social systems—where did they come from?

Individual societies begin in harmonious adaptation to the environment and, like individuals, quickly get trapped into nonadaptive, artificial, repetitive sequences.

When the individual's behavior and consciousness get hooked to a routine sequence of external actions, he is a dead robot, and

When the individual's behavior and consciousness get hooked to a routine sequence of external actions, he is a dead robot, and

When the individual's behavior and consciousness get hooked to a routine sequence of external actions, he is a dead robot, and it is time for him to die and be reborn. Time to "drop out," "turn on," and "tune in." This period of robotization is called the Kali Yuga, the Age of Strife and Empire, the peak of so-called civilization, the Johnson Administration, etc. This relentless law of death, life, change is the rhythm of the galaxies and the seasons, the rhythm of the seed. It never stops.

Drop Out. Turn On. Tune In

Drop Out—detach yourself from the external social drama which is as dehydrated and ersatz as TV.

Turn On—find a sacrament which returns you to the temple of God, your own body. Go out of your mind. Get high.

Tune In—be reborn. Drop back in to express it. Start a new sequence of behavior that reflects your vision.

But the sequence must continue. You cannot stand still.

Death. Life. Structure.

D. L. S.
D. L. S. D. L. S. D.
L. S. D. L. S. D. L.
S. D. L. S. D. . . . . .

Any action that is not a conscious expression of the drop-out-turn-on-tune-in-drop-out rhythm is the dead posturing of robot actors on the fake-prop TV studio stage set that is called American reality.

Actions which are conscious expressions of the turn-on, tune-in, drop-out rhythm are religious.

The wise person devotes his life exclusively to the religious search—for therein is found the only ecstasy, the only meaning.

Anything else is a competitive quarrel over (or Hollywood-love sharing of) television studio props.

How to Turn On

To turn on is to detach from the rigid addictive focus on the fake-prop TV studio set and to refocus on the natural energies within the body.

To turn on, you go out of your mind and:

1. Come to your senses—focus on sensory energies.
2. Resurrect your body—focus on somatic energies.
3. Drift down cellular memory tracks beyond the body's space-time—focus on cellular energies.
4. Decode the genetic code.

Note well: at each of these levels (sensory, somatic, cellular, molecular), attention can be directed at energy changes within or without the body. If attention is directed externally during the session, the outside world is experienced in terms of a non-symbolic energy—language focus. Be careful. This can be shocking. The props of the TV studio stage set are suddenly experienced:

1. As sensory (e.g., the room is alive, out of control, exploding with light and sound)
2. As somatic (e.g., the room is alive, undulating with digestive rhythm)
3. As cellular (e.g., all props and actors take on a stylized, mythic, reincarnate hue)
4. As molecular (e.g., all props and actors shimmer impersonally as vibratory mosaics)

Recognition eliminates fear and confusion. To turn on, you need maps and manuals.

To turn on, you must learn how to pray. Prayer is the compass, the gyroscope for centering and stillness.

Turning on is a complex, demanding, frightening, confusing process. It requires diligent yoga.

Turning on requires a guide who can center you at the TV-stage-prop level and at the sensory, somatic, cellular, and molecular levels.

When you turn on, remember: you are not a naughty boy getting high for kicks.

You are a spiritual voyager furthering the most ancient, noble quest of man. When you turn on, you shed the fake-prop TV studio and costume and join the holy dance of the visionaries. You leave LBJ and Bob Hope; you join Lao-tse, Christ, Blake. Never underestimate the sacred meaning of the turn-on.

To turn on, you need a sacrament. A sacrament is a visible external thing which turns the key to the inner doors. A sacrament must bring about bodily changes. A sacrament flips you out of the TV-studio game and harnesses you to the 2-billion-year-old flow inside.

A sacrament which works is dangerous to the establishment which runs the fake-prop TV studio—and to that part of your mind which is hooked to the studio game.

Each TV-prop society produces exactly that body-changing sacrament which will flip out the mind of the society.

Today the sacrament is LSD. New sacraments are coming along.

Sacraments wear out. They become part of the social TV-studio game. Treasure LSD while it still works. In fifteen years it will be tame, socialized, and routine.

How to Tune In

You cannot stay turned on all the time. You cannot stay anyplace all the time. That's a law of evolution. After the revelation it is necessary to drop back in, return to the fake-prop TV studio and initiate small changes which reflect the glory and the meaning of the turn-on. You change the way you move, the way you dress, and you change your corner of the TV-studio society. You begin to look like a happy saint. Your home slowly becomes a shrine. Slowly, gently, you start seed transformations around you. Psychedelic art. Psychedelic style. Psychedelic music. Psychedelic dance.

Suddenly you discover you have dropped out.

How to Drop Out

Drop out means exactly that: drop out.

Most of the activity of most Americans goes into robot performances on the TV-studio stage. Fake. Unnatural. Automatic.

Drop out means detach yourself from every TV drama which is not in the rhythm of the turn-on, tune-in, drop-out cycle.

Quit school. Quit your job. Don't vote. Avoid all politics. Do not waste conscious thinking on TV-studio games. Political choices are meaningless.

To postpone the drop-out is to cop out.

Dismiss your fantasies of infiltrating the social stage-set game. Any control you have over television props is their control over you.

Dismiss the Judaic-Christian-Marxist-puritan-literary-existentialist suggestion that the drop-out is escape and that the conformist cop-out is reality. Dropping out is the hardest yoga of all.

Make your drop-out invisible. No rebellion—please!

To Drop Out, You Must Form Your Own Religion

The drop-out, turn-on, tune-in rhythm is most naturally done in small groups of family members, lovers, and seed friends.

For both psychedelic and legal reasons, you must form your own cult.

The directors of the TV studio do not want you to live a religious life. They will apply every pressure (including prison) to keep you in their game.

Your own mind, which has been corrupted and neurologically damaged by years of education in fake-prop TV-studio games, will also keep you trapped in the game.

A group liberation cult is required.

You must form that most ancient and sacred of human structures—the clan. A clan or cult is a small group of human beings organized around a religious goal.

Remember, you are basically a primate. You are designed by the 2-billion-year blueprint to live in a small band.

You cannot accept the political or spiritual leadership of anyone you cannot touch, con-spire (breathe) with, worship with, get high with.

Your clan must be centered on a shrine and a totem spiritual energy source. To the clan you dedicate your highest loyalty, and to you the clan offers its complete protection.

But the clan must be centered on religious goals. Religion means being tuned in to the natural rhythm. Religion is the turn-on, tune-in, drop-out process.

Because you and your clan brothers are turned on, you will radiate energy. You will attract attention—hostility from the TV establishment, enthusiastic interest from rootless TV actors who wish to join your clan. Everyone basically wants to turn on, tune in, and drop out.

Avoid conflict with the establishment. Avoid recruiting and rapid growth. Preserve clan harmony.

Your clan must be limited to essential friends.

You must guard against the TV power tendency toward ex-p a n s   i   o   n.

Your clan cannot become a mail-order, mass-numbers organization.

The structure of your clan must be cellular.

The center of your religion must be a private, holy place.

The activities of your religion must be limited to the turn-on, tune-in, drop-out sequence. Avoid commitments to TV-studio power games.

You must start your own religion. You are God—but only you can discover and nurture your divinity. No one can start your religion for you.

In particular, those Americans who use psychedelic chemicals—marijuana, peyote, LSD—must appraise their goals and

games realistically. You smoke pot? Good. But why? As part of
your personality game? As part of the American TV-studio
perspective? To enhance your ego? As part of your TV role as
hipster, sophisticate, rebel? Because it is the in-thing to do in
your stage set? Because it is a social-psychological habit? Good.
Keep on. The "pot game" is a fascinating scenario to act out,
the entertaining game of illicit kicks.

There is another way of viewing psychedelic drugs, including
pot: from the perspective of history. For thousands of years the
greatest artists, poets, philosophers, and lovers have used consciousness-expanding substances to turn on, tune in, drop out.
As part of the search for the meaning of life. As tools to reach
new levels of awareness. To see beyond the immediate social
game. For revelation. For light in the darkness of the long
voyage.

Every great burst of activity has grown out of a psychedelic
turn-on. The visionary then rushes back to tune in, to pass on
the message. A new art form. A new mode of expression. He
turns others on. A cult is formed. A new TV stage set is
designed, one that is closer to the family-clan-tribal cell structure of our species.

Do you wish to use marijuana and LSD to get beyond the TV
scenario? To enhance creativity? As catalysts to deepen wisdom?

If so, you will be helped by making explicit the religious
nature of your psychedelic activities. To give meaning to your
own script, to clarify your relationships with others, and to cope
with the present legal setup, you will do well to start your own
religion.

How to Start Your Own Religion

First, decide with whom you will make the voyage of discovery.
If you have a family, certainly you will include them. If you
have close friends, you will certainly want to include them. The
question, with whom do I league for spiritual discovery? is a
fascinating exercise.

Next, sit down with your spiritual companions and put on a page the plan for your trip. Write down and define your:

Goals

Roles

Rituals

Rules

Vocabulary

Values

Space-time locales

Mythic context

Here is an interesting exercise. You will learn a lot about yourself and your companions. You will see where you are and where you are not.

You will find it necessary to be explicit about the way your clan handles authority, responsibility, sexual relations, money, economics, defense, communication.

In short, you are forming not only your own religion but your own natura political unit. This is inevitable because the basic political unit is exactly the same as the basic spiritual grouping—the clan. Did you really believe that church was only where you went for an hour on Sunday morning?

Make your clan unique. Do not slavishly copy the roles and language of other groups. The beauty of cellular life is that each unit is both so incredibly complexly similar and also so unique. The more you understand the infinite complexity of life, the more you treasure both the similarities and the differences. But you have to be turned on to see it. At the level of the studio-prop game, both the similarities and the differences are trivial.

In defining the goal of your religion, you need not use conventional religious language. You don't have to make your spiritual journey sound "religious." Religion cannot be pompous and high-flown. Religion is consciousness expansion, centered in the body and defined exactly the way it sounds best to you. Don't be intimidated by Caesar's Hollywood fake versions of religiosity. If life has a meaning for you beyond the TV-studio game, you are religious. Spell it out.

So write out your own language for the trip: *God* or *evolu-*

tion, acid or *sacrament, guide* or *guru, purgatorial redemption*
or *bad trip, mystic revelation* or *good high.* Say it naturally.

Develop your own rituals and costumes. Robes or gray flannel
suits, amulets or tattoos. You will eventually find yourself
engaged in a series of sacred moments which feel right to you.

Step by step
    all your actions
       will take on a sacra
         mental meaning. Inevit
           ably you will create a ritual
             sequence for each sense organ
               and for each of the basic energy ex
                 changes—eating, bathing, mating, etc.

You must be explicit about the space-time arrangement for
your God game. Each room in your home will contain a shrine.
Your house will not be a TV actor's dressing room but rather a
spiritual center. Regular rhythms of worship will emerge—daily
meditation (turn-on) sessions (with or without marijuana),
and once a week or once a month you will devote a whole day to
turning on. Time your worship to the rhythm of the seasons, to
the planetary calendar.

Spell out on paper explicit plan$ for handling financial
interaction$. Money i$ a completely irrational focu$ for mo$t
We$terner$. A$ $oon a$ your clan member$ detach them$elve$
emotionally from money, you will discover how easy it is to
survive economically. There must be a complete and collabora-
tive pooling of money and work energy. Any $elfi$h holding
back of dollar$ or muscular energy will weaken the clan. Each
clan, as it drops out of the American game, must appraise its
resources and figure out how to barter with other groups. Each
clan will develop its own productivity.

Sexuality is the downfall of most religious cults. Clarity and
honesty are necessary. Karmic accidental differences exist in
people's sexual makeup. Basically, each man is made to mate
with one woman. Heterosexual monogamous fidelity is the only
natural way of sexual union. However, because this is the Kali

Yuga, and because we live in the final stages of a sick society, sexual variations are inevitable.

Your mode of sexual union is the key to your religion. You cannot escape this. The way you ball (or avoid balling) is your central sacramental activity. The sexual proclivity of the clan must be explicit and inflexible. Do not attempt to establish clan relationships with persons of a different sexual persuasion. There is no value judgment here. Sex is sacred. People of like sexual temperament must form their own spiritual cults. Homosexuality is not an illness. It is a religious way of life. Homosexuals should accept their state as a religious path. Homosexuals cannot join heterosexual clans. Homosexuals should treasure, glorify, their own sexual yoga. Their right to pursue their sacred bodily yoga is guaranteed to them. Heterosexual clans can support, help, learn from, teach homosexual clans, but the difference must be preserved—with mutual respect.

Some spiritual people are not compatible with the monogamous union and prefer a freer sexual regime, the group marriage. Good! Many tribes and clans throughout the planet have flourished in complete and holy promiscuity. But be explicit. Painful confusions occur if sexual orientations and sexual taboos (cellular and physical, not psychological or cultural) are disregarded in forming clans.

Select clan members who share or complement your style, your way of tuning in, your temperament, your sexual orientation.

The aim of clan living is to subordinate the ego game to the family game—the clan game.

You will do well to have an explicit connection to a mythic figure. You must select a historical psychedelic guide. You must know your mythic origins. Facts and news are reports from the current TV drama. They have no relevance to your 2-billion-year-old divinity. Myth is the report from the cellular memory bank. Myths humanize the recurrent themes of evolution.

You select a myth as a reminder that you are part of an ancient and holy process. You select a myth to guide you when you drop out of the narrow confines of the fake-prop studio set.

Your mythic guide must be one who has solved the death-rebirth riddle. A TV drama hero cannot help you. Caesar, Napoleon, Kennedy are no help to your cellular orientation. Christ, Lao-tse, Hermes Trismegistus, Socrates are recurrent turn-on figures.

You will find it absolutely necessary to leave the city. Urban living is spiritually suicidal. The cities of America are about to crumble as did Rome and Babylon. Go to the land. Go to the sea.

Psychedelic centers located in cities will serve as collecting areas. Thousands of spiritual seekers are coming to urban districts where they meet in meditation centers and psychedelic assembly places.* There they form their clans. They migrate from the city.

The Legal Question

Unless you form your own new religion and devote an increasing amount of your energies to it, you are (however exciting your personality TV role) a robot. Your new religion can be formed only by you. Do not wait for a messiah. Do it yourself. Now.

The goals, roles, rules, rituals, values, language, space-tie locale, and mythic context of your religion must be put on paper for two reasons. One, to make the journey clear and explicit for yourself and your clan members, and two, to deal with Caesar.

The relationship between Caesar and the God seeker has

---

* Psychedelic centers are rapidly springing up in metropolitan areas, and this tendency must be encouraged. A simple format for a psychedelic enterprise may involve a shop front with a meditation room in the rear. Numerous shops calling themselves "psychedelic" are springing up throughout the country. This development is inevitable, but one should be skeptical about the spiritual nature of such commercial enterprises unless they include a meditation room. Psychedelic businesses should support spiritual communities and provide centers for clan formation.

always been uneasy. But the boundaries of the tension can be defined precisely, and if you are clear in your mind, there can be no confusion. You can move with exactness and confidence.

Everything that exists outside your body and your shrine belongs to Caesar. Caesar has constructed the fake-prop studio for his king-of-the-mountain game, and he can have it. Highways, property, status, power, money, weapons, all things, all external man-made objects belong to him. The spiritual life is completely detached from these props. Obey Caesar's TV studio rules when you are in his studios. Avoid any participation in his dramas.

But remember, your body is the kingdom of heaven, and your home is the shrine in which the kingdom of heaven is to be found. What you do inside your body, what energies you let contact your sense organs, and what you put into your body is your business.*

All you need do to protect the divinity of your body and the sanctity of your shrine is to be explicit—and to worship with dignity and courage.

Write down an eightfold definition of your religion (goal, role, rule, ritual, value, language, myth, space-time locale). By doing so, you have formed your religion. The First Amendment to the Constitution, the charter of the UN, and the ancient traditions of human history give you protection to alter your own consciousness inside your shrine.

If you take a psychedelic sacrament, leave your house and commit a disorder on Caesar's streets; let him arrest you for overt crime. But your right to turn on in your home is sacred. You make your home a shrine by writing it into the charter of your religion.

In writing your charter, you must specify where you will take the sacrament and with whom. The charter does not permit you to turn on anywhere. You must respect the possessive claims of Caesar to his fake-front stage sets. And you must also specify visible objects of worship which will be found in your shrine—a

* You are God: Remember!

statue of Buddha, a picture of Christ, a rock, a wooden carving. You choose, but be explicit.

Get your charter notarized, or mail it to yourself in a post-marked envelope. You have thereby established, before possible conflict with Caesar's police, your religion. These are the mini-mum steps required to protect your use of psychedelic drugs. If you don't care enough to do this, you don't care enough.

But further steps are preferable. It is highly advisable, and quite simple, to incorporate your religion under the laws of your state. Consult a lawyer—a psychedelic lawyer if possible. There are thousands of them around. How? Well, he'll be under the age of thirty. Your local ACLU would be a good place to start. Ask him to file incorporation papers which are standard and which every lawyer has in mimeographed outline.

Follow the simple steps necessary to complete the forms, and in short order, you are a legally incorporated religion. Your own sense of dignity and commitment to the spiritual life is encouraged. Your posture and confidence vis-à-vis Caesar's Key-stone Kops is immeasurably strengthened.

But you must play it straight. Don't sign anything you aren't going to live up to. On the other hand, leave room in your charter for easy revision of your religious practices. You are a young, growing religion. For God's sake, don't get caught in rigidities at the beginning.

Use psychedelic sacraments only in designated shrines and only with members of a psychedelic religion. If you are going to be naughty and smoke pot in the washroom of one of Caesar's stage sets, why that's all right—but be clear; you waive your religious rights. Do what you will, but be conscious and don't mix up your naughty game with your religious game.

After you have incorporated your religion, you can file the application forms and a description of methods of worship in the attorney's office. In case of any misunderstanding with Caesar's cops, you will be effectively prepared. Don't be sur-prised at the idea of having a lawyer to handle your psychedelic affairs. Psychedelic lawyers will be the most numerous and popular segment of the legal profession in 15 years. For a small amount of money you can have ongoing legal protection for your religion. You'd do it for your business, wouldn't you? It's better yet if you find a lawyer who is ready to join your clan.*

There is a third legal step which many psychedelic religionists will want to take—the licensing for the importation and distribution of illegal sacraments such as marijuana and LSD. The legal procedure involved in obtaining permission to use drugs is called a declaratory judgment. This procedure can result in a court declaration that an individual or a group may, with the sanction of law, use drugs freely for religious purposes.

In requesting a declaratory judgment to import and distribute illegal sacraments (and remember here that alcohol, nicotine, and automobiles are also illegal—except to licensed operators), you are asking nothing more than was permitted to Catholic priests and Jewish rabbis during alcohol prohibition. These religionists were allowed to import and distribute an illegal drug—booze—for distribution only by priests and only in designated shrines. The quarter of a million members of the Native American Church are similarly licensed to use peyote, a plant much more powerful than marijuana.

The filing for a declaratory judgment requires more commitment and energy—and thus becomes the third test of your religious stamina. How much do you care?

By the end of 1968 we expect that thousands of such applications will be flooding the courts. In each case, the decision as to whether the applicants are entitled to a license to smoke marijuana and use LSD will have to be made on the merits of the case. Each judge and jury will have to rule on the sincerity of the applicants. What a wonderful exercise! Thousands of groups of young Americans will choose to present and defend their new religions in the courts. What a beautiful forum for free debate on the values of marijuana as opposed to booze!

Thousands of jury members and hundreds of judges will be converted.

In all of these activities there is no hostility, no competition, no conflict with Caesar. Love and humor are the means. The ends will follow.

---

* Your lawyer can write to the League for Spiritual Discovery for further legal information, relevant briefs, precedents, etc.

Dr. Leary, What Will Happen to Society After Everyone
Turns On, Tunes In, and Drops Out?

An interesting indication of the "miraculous" growth of LSD comes in the form of the question: What will happen to society after everyone turns on, tunes in, and drops out?

At the surface, the question seems naïve. Nowhere and never does everyone do the same thing at the same time. It's all planned in cycles by the DNA code. Organic changes occur gradually and invisibly.

This question reflects the sudden panic of the TV bit player. What will happen to me if the show goes off the air? Will I lose my little part? What an incomparable tragedy if these cardboard studio walls were to fall down!

The emotional response to this game terror is reassurance. Don't worry. Your life begins when your TV game ends. Turn on, tune in, drop out. Then you are free to walk out of the studio—a god in the Garden of Eden.

The intellectual answer to the question is infinitely complex, depending upon how much time and energy one can mobilize for utopian planning. The League for Spiritual Discovery has worked out detailed blueprints for the next cycle of man's social evolution. Future manuals will be published by the league describing the year-by-year unfolding.

In summary: be prepared for a complete change of American urban technology. Grass will grow in Times Square within ten years. The great soil-murdering lethal skyscrapers will come down. Didn't you know they were stage sets? Didn't you know they had to come down? The transition will come either violently (by war) or gently, aesthetically, through a psychedelic drop-out process.

In any case, there is nothing for you to do in a collective political sense. Turn on, tune in, drop out. Discover and nurture your own divinity and that of your friends and family members.

Center on your clan and the natural order will prevail.

2

*American Education as an Addictive Process and Its Cure**

The topic is the individual in the college, his commitments and his work. A broad subject indeed! Let us define the task more specifically. Let's aim the dialogue to each of you, who are, after all, individuals in the college. Let's talk directly and prophetically to your situation.

Let's set an ambitious goal to present the most important message you have ever listened to, to present a challenge which will change some of your lives. This may sound immodest but it's not, really, because what we shall consider has nothing to do with me personally. Like the other speakers, I, too, have been sent over by Central Casting to read my lines in the scenario we are working on today. I am simply a temporary mouthpiece for the message you are about to hear. Another reason for setting a bold goal is that this is my last performance in this particular drama. This is my last lecture as a college teacher to a college audience, and after the performance I'm going to take off the greasepaint and change uniform and move on to another show.

The third reason for claiming that my ambition today is not immodest is that I am saying nothing new. I didn't write the

---

* This chapter is a revision of a lecture given by Dr. Timothy Leary at the Second Annual Symposium on American Values, Central Washington State College, Ellensburg, Washington, April 1963. One week following the lecture, the speaker was fired from Harvard University for being absent from class, a paradoxical charge since his regularly scheduled courses had been assigned to other professors the preceding September.

script. The lines were written by the oldest playwright in the business I am simply repeating the oldest message in human history. We know, of course, that the wise men don't talk. The Book of Tao tells us that he who knows, speaks not and he who speaks, knows not. When the wise men in the past did talk, they have always written the same book. They have always told us the same message, repeated in a different dialect, using the metaphor of their time, using the vocabulary of their tribe, but it is always the same message. "Turn off your mind. Step for a moment or two out of your own ego. Stop your robot activity for a while. Stop the game you are in. Look within."

Oh, words! More good advice! The words that I have just given you are pretty trite and cliché today in the twentieth century, aren't they? But 3,000 years ago, when they were first enunciated, they were tremendously exciting. They probably brought about biochemical changes in the neurosystems of the people that heard these chants for the first time. Of course, now in the twentieth century, we are bombarded by words, thousands of words an hour, so that what I've just said is only another tattoo of syllables bouncing off your ears. Today we don't know what to look for if we try to get out of our game, and we don't know how to do it.

Now if you look at some of the metaphors that were used by these men in the past who changed the course of human history, the great visionaries, the great religious leaders, the great poets, you find an interesting correlation, a similarity. They all found the same thing when they looked within. They talked about the inner light, about the soul, the divine flame, the spark, or the seed of life, or the white light of the void. You will recognize that I have just ranged in these metaphors through several great philosophers, both Eastern and Western. All of these metaphors rang true and were right at the time. We can recognize now that they were clumsy metaphors for what are actually physiological processes within our nervous system. Listen! Each of those poetic images within the next 2 to 5 years is going to be validated by modern biochemistry and modern pharmacology.

Let me define the problem as I see it. I want to define it first of all ontologically, in the scientific sense, and then later I'll talk about the social aspects of the problem which we now face.

Ontologically there are an infinite number of realities, each one defined by the particular space-time dimension which you use. From the standpoint of one reality, we may think that the other realities are hallucinatory, or psychotic, or far out, or mysterious, but that is just because we're caught at the level of one space-time perception.

For many people it's an infuriating thought that there are many, many realities. Last week, I was giving a lecture on consciousness expansion with Professor Alpert at the Aero-Space Institute in Los Angeles. A young engineer happened to be in the building that night, busy with some aerospace activity, and as he was leaving the building, he saw this crowd in a large room, and he came in to listen. After the lecture was over and we were on the way out, he stopped us and started to argue about reality. He could hardly talk, he was so mad. He said, "There is only one reality, the reality that is here, the reality of our physical laws, and for you to say that there is a range of realities, and particularly to say that this range might be brought about by drugs, is intellectual fraud, deceiving your fellow man!" It seemed to disturb him and make him angry to think that this solidity (which we are convinced exists around us) is perhaps just one level of an enormously complex continuum of realities. Now it's bad enough to say that there are other realities, but it's really intolerable if we suggest that some of the other realities are more conducive to ecstasy, happiness, wisdom, to more effective activity, than our familiar reality. So much for the general ontological situation. Let us try to spell this out in more exact terms.

The social reality in which we have been brought up and which we have been taught to perceive and deal with is a fairly gross and static affair. But it misses the real excitement. The real hum and drama, the beauty of the electronic, cellular, somatic, sensory energy process have no part in our usual picture of reality. We can't see the life process. We are surrounded by it all the time. It is exploding inside of us in a billion cells in our body, but most of the time we can't experience it. We are blind to it. For example, how do we know when another person is alive? We have to poke his robot body and listen to his heart, look for some movement. If he breathes, he is alive. But that is not the life process. That is just the external symptom. It's like seeing that the car moves, and from the fact that the body of the car moves, inferring that the motor is going inside. We can hear the car motor, we can brake, but we can't tune in on the machinery of life inside ourselves or around us. Now at this point you must be thinking, well, poor Leary, he has gone too far out. But really I don't think that it should be this difficult to accept logically the fact that there are many realities and that the most exciting things that happen, cellular and nuclear processes, the manufacture of protein from DNA blueprints, are not at the level of our routine perception. And for that matter, that the most complex communications, the most creative processes, exist at levels of which we are not ordinarily aware.

Let's take an analogy. Suppose that you had never heard of the microscope, and I came before you and said, "Ladies and gentlemen, I have an instrument which brings into view an entirely different picture of reality, according to which this world around us which seems to have solidity and symmetry and certain form is actually made up of organisms, each of which is a universe; there is a world inside a drop of water. A drop of blood is like a galaxy. A leaf is a fantastic organization perhaps more complicated than our own social structure." You would think that I was pretty far out, until that moment when I could persuade you to put your eye down to the microscope, show you how to focus, and then you would share the wonder which I had tried to communicate to you. All right, we know that cellular activity is infinitely complex.

We tend to think of our external, leatherlike skin body as the basic ontological frame of reference. The center of our universe. This foolish egocentricity becomes apparent when we compare our body with a tractor. We usually think of a tractor or a harvesting machine as a clumsy, crude instrument which just organizes and brings food for us to feed our mouths. But from the standpoint of the cell, the animal's body, the human being's body, your body, is a clumsy instrument, the function of which is to transport the necessary supplies to keep the cellular life process going. And we realize, when we study biology textbooks, that our body is actually a complex set of soft-divine machines serving in myriad ways the needs of the cell. These concepts can be a little disturbing to our egocentric and our anthropocentric point of view.

But then we've just started, because the fellow with the electron microscope comes along. And he says, "Well, your microscope and your cell is nothing! Sure, the cell is complicated, but there's a whole universe inside the atom in which activities move with the speed of light, and talk about excitement, talk about fun, talk about communication, well, now here at the electron level we're just getting into it." And then the astronomer comes along with his instruments, and off we go again!

The interesting thing to me about this new vision of many realities that science confronts us with (however unwilling we are to look at it) is this: the closer and closer connection between the cosmology of modern science and the cosmology of some of the Eastern religions, in particular, Hinduism and Buddhism. I have a strong suspicion that within the next few years, we are going to see many of the hypotheses of our Christian mystics and many of the cosmological and ontological theories of Eastern philosophers spelled out objectively in biochemical terms. Now, all of these phenomena "out there" made visible by the electron microscope, the telescope, are wounding enough to our pride and our anthropomorphism (which Robert Ardry calls the "romantic fallacy"), but here, perhaps the most disturbing of all, comes modern pharmacology. Now we have evidence which suggests that by ingesting a tiny bit of substance which will change biochemical balances inside our nervous system, it's possible to experience directly some of the things which we externally view through the lenses of the microscope.

I will have more to say about the applications and implications of educational chemistry shortly. I'd like to stop and consider briefly the social-political and educational problems which are the subject of our symposium. We have told each other over and over again during the last two days of the conference that we're in pretty bad shape. Well, I'm not quite that pessimistic. What's in bad shape? The cellular process isn't in bad shape. The supreme intelligence, if you want to use that corny twentieth-century phrase for the DNA molecule, isn't in bad shape. For that matter, the human species is going to survive, probably in some mutated form. What's in bad shape? Our social games. Our secular traditions, our favorite concepts, our cultural systems. These transitory phenomena are collapsing and will have to give way to more advanced evolutionary products.

I'm very optimistic about the cellular process and the human species because they are part, we are part of the fantastic rushing flow which has been pounding along from one incredible climax to another for some 2 billion years. And you can't stay back there, hanging on to a rock in the stream. You've got to go along with the flow; you've got to trust the process, and you've got to adapt to it, and you might as well try to understand it and enjoy it. I have some suggestions in a moment as to how to do exactly that.

We are all caught in a social situation which is getting increasingly set and inflexible and frozen. A social process which is hanging on to a rock back there somewhere and keeping us from flowing along with the process. All the classic symptoms are there: professionalism, bureaucracy, reliance and overreliance on the old clichés, too much attention to the external and material, the uniformity and conformity caused by mass communication. The old drama is repeating itself. It happened in Rome and it happened to the Persian Empire and the Turkish Empire and it happened in Athens. The same symptoms. We're caught in what seems like an air-conditioned anthill, and we see that we're drifting helplessly toward war, overpopulation, plastic stereotyping. We're diverted by our circuses—the space race and television—but we're getting scared, and what's worse, we're getting bored and we're ready for a new page in the story. The next evolutionary step.

And what is the next step? Where is the new direction to be found? The wise men have been telling us for 3,000 years: it's going to come from *within,* from within your head.

The human being, we know, is a very recent addition to the animal kingdom. Sometime around 70,000 years ago (a mere fraction of a second in terms of the evolutionary time scale), the erect primate with the large cranium seems to have appeared. In a sudden mutational leap the size of the skull and the brain is swiftly doubled. A strange cerebral explosion. According to one paleo-neurological theory (Dr. Tilly Edinger), "Enlargement of the cerebral hemisphere by 50 percent seems to have taken place without having been accompanied by any major increase in body size."

Thus we come to the fascinating possibility that man, in the short infancy of his existence, has never learned to use this new neurological machinery. That perhaps, like a child turned loose in the control room of a billion-tube computer, man is just beginning to catch on to the idea, just beginning to discover that there is an infinity of meaning and complex power in the equipment he carries around behind his own eyebrows.

The first intimation of this incredible situation was given by Alfred Russel Wallace, co-discoverer with Charles Darwin of what we call the theory of evolution. Wallace was the first to point out that the so-called savage—the Eskimo, the African tribesman—far from being an offshoot of a primitive and never-developed species, had the same neural equipment as the literate European. He just wasn't using it the same way. He hadn't developed it linguistically and in other symbolic game sequences. "We may safely infer," said Wallace, "that the savage possesses a brain capable, if cultivated and developed, of performing work of a kind and degree far beyond what he is ever required to do." We shall omit discussion of the ethnocentric assumptions (Protestant ethic, primitive-civilized) which are betrayed in this quote and follow the logic to its next step.

Here we face the embarrassing probability that the same is true of us. In spite of our mechanical sophistication we may well be savages, simple brutes quite unaware of the potential within. It is highly likely that coming generations will look back at us and wonder: how could they so childishly play with their simple toys and primitive words and remain ignorant of the speed, power, and relational potential within? How could they fail to use the equipment they possessed?

According to Loren Eiseley (whose argument I have been following in the last few paragraphs), "When these released potentialities for brain growth began, they carried man into a new world where the old laws no longer held. With every advance in language, in symbolic thought, the brain paths multiplied. Significantly enough, these which are most recently acquired and less specialized regions of the brain, the 'silent areas,' mature last. Some neurologists, not without reason, suspect that here may lie other potentialities which only the future of the race may reveal."

We are using, then, a very small percentage of the neural equipment, the brain capacity which we have available. We perceive and act at one level of reality when there are any number of places, any number of directions in which we can move.

Ladies and gentlemen, it is time to wake up! It's time to really use our heads. But how? Let's consider our topic: the individual in college. Can the college help us use our heads? To think about the function of the college, we have to think about the university as a place which spawns new ideas or breaks through to new visions. A place where we can learn how to use our neurological equipment.

The university, and for that matter, every aspect of the educational system, is paid for by adult society to train young people to keep the same game going. To be sure that you do not use your heads. Students, this institution and all educational institutions are set up to anesthetize you, to put you to sleep. To make sure that you will leave here and walk out into the bigger game and take your place in the line. A robot like your parents, an obedient, efficient, well-adapted social game player. A replaceable part in the machine.

Now you *are* allowed to be a tiny bit rebellious. You can have fancy ways of dress, you can become a cute teen-ager, you can have panty raids, and that sort of thing. There is a little leeway to let you think that you are doing things differently. But don't let that kid you.

I looked at television last night for a few minutes and watched a round table of high school students discussing problems. Very serious social problems. They were discussing teenage drinking. Now the problem seems to be that young people want to do the grown-up things a little too fast. You want to start using the grown-ups' narcotics before you're old enough. Well, don't be in such a hurry! You'll be doing the adult drinking pretty soon. You'll be performing all the other standardized adult robot sequences because that is what they're training you to do. The last thing that an institution of education wants to allow you to do is to expand your consciousness, to use the untapped potential in your head, to experience directly. They don't want you to evolve, to grow, to really grow. They don't want you to move on to a different level of reality. They don't want you to take life seriously, they want you to take their game seriously. Education, dear students, is anesthetic, a narcotic procedure which is very likely to blunt your sensitivity and to immobolize your brain and your behavior for the rest of your lives.

I also would like to suggest that our educational process is an especially dangerous narcotic because it probably does direct physiological damage to your nervous system. Let me explain what I mean by that. Your brain, like any organ of your body, is a perfect instrument. When you were born, you brought into the world this organ which is almost perfectly adapted to sense what is going on around you and inside of you. Just as the heart knows its job, your brain is ready to do its job. But what education does to your head would be like taking your heart and wrapping rubber bands around it and putting springs on it to make sure it can pump. What education does is to put a series of

filters over your awareness so that year by year, step by step, you
experience less and less and less. A baby, we're convinced, sees
much more than we do. A kid of ten or twelve is still playing
and moving around with some flexibility. But an adult has
filtered experience down to just the plastic reactions. This is a
biochemical phenomenon. There's considerable evidence showing that a habit is a neural network of feedback loops. Like
grooves in a record, like muscles, the more you use any one of
the loops, the more likely you are to use it again. If there were
time, I could spell out exactly how this conditioning process,
this educational process, works, how it is based on early, accidental, imprinted emotions.

So here we are once again. The monolithic, frozen empire is
about to fall. We have been in this position many times in the
last few thousand years. What can we do about educational
narcosis? How can you "kick" the conformist habit? How can
you learn to use your head?

We're all caught in this social addictive process. You young
people know that it's not working out the way it could. You
know you're hooked. You dread the robot sequence. But there
is always the promise, isn't there? There's always the come-on.
"Keep coming. It's going to get better. Something great is going
to happen tomorrow if you're good today." It's not! As a matter
of fact, it gets worse, dear robots.

All right, where do we go? What can we do? I have two
answers to those questions. The first is: *drop out!* Go out
where you are closer to reality, to direct experience. Go out to
where things are really happening. Go out to the frontier. Go
out to those focal points where important issues are being
played out. Why don't you pick out the most important problem in the world, as you see it, and go exactly to the center of
the place where it's happening, where it is being studied and
worked on? Why not? Someone has to be there, in the center.
Why not you?

Now, there's a risk to this. The first risk is that you'll lose
your foothold on the ladder that you've been climbing. You'll
lose your social connection.

Undergraduates come to me very often and say, "I want to go on to graduate school in psychology. Where should I go?" And I always ask them the question, "Why do you want to study psychology?" And as I listen to them, usually one of two answers develops. Answer number one is: "I want to become a psychologist. I want to play the psychology game. I want to be able to play the role and use the terms you use, and I want to be an assistant professor and then an associate professor and then a full professor, and I want to get tenure, and maybe if I'm really ambitious, I might get to be president of the American Psychological Association." Well, that's fair enough, and for someone who has that ambition I can give them advice about the strategic universities to go to, like go to Michigan or Yale but don't go to XYZ.

Some students, though, will say, "I want to study psychology because I want to study human nature" or "I want to find out what's what." To do some good. And then I can tell them, well, forget about graduate school. What kind of good do you want to do? Do you want to help the mentally ill? Then get yourself committed to a mental hospital. Stay there for a year or two; you'll learn more about mental illness in that two years than our profession has learned in a hundred years. If you want to learn about delinquency and reducing crime, go down to the tough section, learn the crime game, learn how to make a man-to-man contact with tough guys, learn from them why they are crooks and criminals. Spend a year in prison, not as a psychologist, but maybe as a guard, or cleaning up the garbage, and you'll learn more than you will ever learn in a criminology textbook. That is how it goes. There is no problem that can't be best solved and best worked out at this stage of ignorance by getting right into the reality.

Of course, another objection to this suggestion is: "After all, we do need some information and we do need facts and we have to learn them in university courses." And I say, "Sure, there are existential problems; there are certain times when in trying to solve an existential problem you will want to borrow the experience and the data of previous investigators." You can use the library, but again, beware, it's just like a narcotic. Library books are very dangerous addictive substances. Like heroin, books become an end in themselves. I made the suggestion two years ago at Harvard University that they lock up Widener Library, put chains on the doors, and have little holes in the wall like in bank tellers' windows, and if a student wanted to get a book, he would have to come with a little slip made out showing that he had some existential, practical question. He wouldn't say that he wanted to stuff a lot of facts in his mind so that he could impress a teacher or be one up on the other students in the intellectual game. No. But if he had an existential problem, then the library would help him get all the information that could be brought to bear on that problem. Needless to say, this plan didn't make much of a hit, and the doors of the Harvard Library are still open. You can still get dangerous narcotic volumes without a prescription at Harvard.

Where can we go?

Answer number one is to get out into the world, go to where the really important events, the events that you think are important, are happening and climb into them. That, by the way, is how all the great advances in science as well as politics have taken place.

Answer number two to the question, where can we go, is: Go inside. Go into your own brain; start using the untapped region of your head. Here, my friends, is the real frontier, the real challenge, the real opportunity.

Well, how do we do that? For centuries, for thousands of years, men have been studying this problem of how to expand their own consciousness, how to get into their own brains. One of the classic methods of doing it is the simple process of meditation. But today in 1963 this method seems far out. You'd be called eccentric if you said to an American that it would be useful for him to spend one hour a day alone—not thinking but just turning off all of the outside stimulation and the internal mental machinery and seeing where that will take him. We have to remind ourselves that meditation has been the classic psychological technique for thousands of years for most of the human race. Every one of our great visionaries, every one of the men who changed the course of human history, worked it out during a meditative experience.

Modern psychology calls this "turning on" by the fancy name "sensory deprivation." A few years ago psychologists discovered that if you took an American and you put him in a dark room and you cut off all the sound and you cut off all the light and you cut off all tactile stimulation, in other words, if you turned off all the outside games, he couldn't keep his mind going and strange things would take place in his consciousness and he would begin to have hallucinations, revelations, visions, or he'd get in a panic and leap out of the room and shout "Help!" The reason for this is (and now we are getting back into neuropsychology) that your mind, your game-playing verbal mind, like a drug habit, requires continual stimulation. You have to keep feeding it. In order to keep up the pretense that you are you and that your level of reality is really reality, you have to have feedback all the time. You have to have people around you reminding you that you are you; you have to have people around you participating in the same immediate realities, sharing the same social delusion, to keep this social reality going.

Now whenever you get out there, away from the social and sensory stimulation (as with men who are shipwrecked, men who are lost in a desert, men who are lost in the snow, men who go into monasteries, men who go into cells), there are withdrawal symptoms. The people panic because they are moving on to a different level of reality. How many of our great visionaries, our great history-making decisions, have come from men who have gone off in the desert? Jesus Christ went off in a cave in the mountain; Mohammed sat alone in a cave; Buddha lived in solitude for many years, so did St. John of the Cross. So have most of our other great visionaries. The problem now is that it is getting harder to let these physiological events happen. To be alone in order to look within.

Recently our technology, which has done so much to narrow our consciousness and to produce this robotlike conformity, has turned up two very disturbing processes which are going to cause all of us to do a lot of serious thinking in the next few years. These processes are electrical stimulation of the brain, and the new drugs, which also allow for increased control of consciousness, either by you or by someone else. The next evolutionary step is going to come through these two means, both of which involve greater knowledge, greater control, greater use and application of that major portion of our brain which we now do not use and of which we are only dimly aware.

These potentialities and these promises aren't going to go away. Your head, with its unused neurons, is there. Electrical stimulation and biochemical expansion of the neural processes are here, too. They aren't going to go away just because they upset our theories of psychology or our new words of education.

In 1943, a most dramatic event took place in a laboratory in Switzerland when Dr. Albert Hoffman accidentally ingested a tiny amount of semisynthetic ergot fungus known as LSD 25 and found himself thrown onto a level of reality which he had never experienced before. This had probably happened to many chemists in the past and to many other people in the past. Hoffman was the man on the spot who was able to understand what was going on. And because of Albert Hoffman of Sandoz Laboratory, we face today the challenge and dilemma of consciousness-expanding drugs. They are not addictive in the sense that there is no physiological attachment to them. I must point out that the very question of addiction is humorous to those of us that feel that we are all hopelessly addicted to words and to our tribal games. These drugs are physiologically safe. Over two thousand studies have been published, and as of 1968 despite the rumors there is no evidence of somatic or physical side effects. But they are *dangerous;* the sociopolitical dangers are there. We have incontrovertible evidence that these drugs cause panic, poor judgment, and irrational behavior on the part of some college deans, psychiatrists and government administrators *who have not taken them.*

What we think is going to happen is that a system of licensing and training will be developed, very similar to the way we train

and license people to use motorcars and airplanes. People have
to demonstrate that they can use their expanded neural machinery without hurting themselves and without danger to their
fellow men. They will have to demonstrate proficiency, experience, training, and then we feel it is their right to be licensed.
As in the case of airplane and auto, the license can be taken
away from those who injure themselves or injure their fellow
men.

There are many new by-products of this research in consciousness expansion and these studies. First of all, it is inevitable that a new language will develop to communicate the new
aspect of experience. The language of words we now use is
extremely clumsy, static, and heavy. We are going to have to
develop, as chemistry has developed, a language that will pay
respect to the fact that our experience, our behavior, our social
forms are flowing all the time. And if your language isn't
equipped to change and flow with them, then you are in
trouble, you're hooked. You're drugged by the educational
system. There are going to be new values, rest assured, based on
a broader range of reality. Our present values, based on certain
ethnocentric tribal goals, are going to recede in importance
after we see where man really belongs in the biological evolutionary process. There are going to be new social forms; there
are going to be new methods of education.

I'll give you one example here. In the last few months, we
have been studying accelerated learning by the use of the
expanded consciousness. It's your trained mind, you remember,
which prevents you from learning. If a professor of linguistics
who doesn't know any French goes to France with his five-year-
old son and they both spend equal time with the French people,
who is going to learn French faster? The five-year-old son will
quickly outstrip his dad even with that Ph.D. in linguistics.
Why? Because Dad has stuffed his mind with all sorts of censor-
ing and filtering concepts that prevent him from grooving with
the French process. The psychedelic experience can release
these learning blocks. We took, for example, a brilliant woman
who had an emotional block against learning language. She

wanted to learn Spanish. We gave her a very heavy dose of LSD, put her in a quiet room and put earphones on her, and for eight hours she was flooded with spoken Spanish from records. Every hour or so, we would go in and take the earphones off and say, "How are you?" She answered ecstatically in Spanish! She had been wallowing in Spanish for a thousand years. By the sixth or seventh hour, she was repeating back the Spanish words with the right enunciation, the dialectic tempo and so forth. The problem now is that when she hears Spanish spoken, she is likely to go into another level of consciousness, to get suddenly very high, which leads to other interesting possibilities of auto-conditioning. All of us, adults and students, have been censored so much, the filters have been applied for so long, the neuro-physiological processes are so firmly set that if we want to expand our consciousness, we are probably going to have to use chemical means. We adults, if we are going to move on to different levels of reality, are going to have to rely on some direct means of this sort. We have high hopes for the next generation, and particularly the next generation after that. It is the goal of our research and of our educational experiments that in one or two generations, we will be witnessing the appearance of human beings who have much more access, without drugs, to a much greater percentage of their nervous systems.

So there you have it. I'm sure that a few or none of you will follow the advice and the prophetic warnings that I have been giving. I have had to tell you with words. But I'm also going to take my own advice. I'm dropping out of the university and educational setup. I'm breaking the habit. I hope in the coming years as you drift into somnambulance that some of you will remember our meeting this morning and will break your addiction to the system. I'll be waiting for you.

I want to leave one final warning. There will be many people who will see the utility of the electrical and chemical techniques I have been talking about and will want to use them, as the Western, scientific mind has always wanted to use them, for their own power and their own control. Whenever new frontiers open up, you have the new problem of exploitation and selfish use. There will be no lack of people who will be delighted to use the underdeveloped areas of *your* cortex. We have coined the term "internal freedom." It is a political, didactic device; we want to warn you not to give up the freedom which you may not even know you have. In the Seattle paper yesterday, in one of the columns, I read a very interesting item to the effect that the Russians were developing extrasensory-perception techniques and studying ways which can eventually control consciousness. We can do that, of course, with television now. If 60 million people all watch one program, they are being controlled. But still we have that choice of turning it on or off. The next step, and I warn you it is not far off, involves some fellow using electrical implants and drugs to control consciousness. Then, dear friends, it may be too late. We won't know where the buttons are to turn them off. The open access to these methods is the key to internal freedom. If we know what we are doing, do it openly and collaboratively, free from government control, then we will be free to explore the tremendous worlds which lie within.

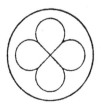

SEAL OF THE LEAGUE

3

Soul Session[*]

SoL: As a former professor at Harvard University, and at the time before the experiments with hallucinogens came up, a recognized figure in the field of psychology, you seem to have had a radical about-face when you started talking recently about "drop out, turn on, and tune in." Would you explain to us what you mean by this?

LEARY: Well, to begin with, I don't think I've made any radical about-face. My use of the psychedelic chemicals stems directly from my endeavors in psychology. I have found better ways of understanding man's consciousness leading to a better control of his inner environment. The techniques of modern psychiatry and psychology don't do this. In my search for new methods, I was led to the study of the drug.

SoL: From being a member ostensibly of the academic in-group, you seemed to have evolved an "in" beyond that.

LEARY: If you study the careers of men that are the central figures in our culture, and I'm not saying I am one, but I model myself after them, you will find that as they pursue their data they get further and further removed from Main Street moral-ity and from the dogmas of the academy. Anyone who takes his work seriously has to expect that he will be led into that frightening and insecure area on the fringe. If he doesn't want to be led out of his mind, he must look at himself in the mirror

---

*This interview was conducted by Ken Garrison, editor of *SOL* magazine, Valley State College, California.

and realize that he is not a true scientist—he's playing the game of the academy and academic corrosion. Far from being unconventional, I see my unfolding as highly orthodox and predictable for anyone who takes truth and knowledge seriously.

SOL: It was my understanding you were dismissed from Harvard for continuing psychedelic experiments on or with students there at the college. Would you explain the circumstances under which you left?

LEARY: One cannot ever believe what you hear in the newspapers. I was not fired by Harvard for giving drugs to undergraduates. I never gave drugs to any undergraduate at Harvard. I had been offered tenure from Harvard twice under the condition that I stop doing research or tone down the research of LSD. I refused to do this. I didn't want to be a professor at Harvard, I wanted to find out where it's at and what's what, and you usually can't always do that at a university.

SOL: Were you simply not granted tenure, and therefore you had to leave the college? We have a very similar circumstance at Valley State. An instructor has been there past the time that you either have to be granted tenure or you have to leave. Is that—?

LEARY: No, the technicality on which I was fired with only two months to go on my salary, on my contract, was because I was absent from classes.

SOL: If you had the opportunity to—

LEARY: I was absent from all my classes because they had taken all my classes away from me. [*Laughter*] So I left, and they knew I was leaving.

SOL: If you had the opportunity to practice the psychedelic research which you are engaged in now, would you accept a position at an American college or university?

LEARY: Absolutely not. I consider American education to be a highly dangerous, addictive, contracting process. I'm quite serious about this, and I urge all students at every level of education to drop out. You're going to learn very little of value and meaning in high school and college, and your mind is going to be trapped and hooked. We are urging young people to drop out of the very new and radical institution of American education and find a teacher, a tutor, and you learn what is appropriate and relevant.

SOL: In other words, if I interpret you correctly, you are proposing for the millions of students and young people a system of individual, small-clan tutor-learner situations, and that you propose, as far as learning processes go, that this is the form, or rather this is the lack of form it should have?

LEARY: Yes, but let's not take any statement I make out of context. Obviously, when I say the kid shouldn't go to school, I'm implying changes in the broader social fabric of our country which we foresee coming. What we have in the United States today is a typical centralization and urbanization which happened in Rome, which happened in Constantinople, which has happened throughout human history, in which enormous masses of people crowd together in the anonymous robotlike anthill of city life. Now, if you want to be an IBM computer robot or a bit actor in the American television studio of American society, go to school and they'll teach you all the little rules of rote behavior that'll get you right out in the TV studio. If you want to be a machine, go to college. But we are anticipating and predicting a change in our society. There is going to be a return to the basic human unit which is the clan or the cult, or the tribe. What I'm predicting and urging is the most orthodox American model. We try to become self-sufficient rather than depend on government paychecks and Social Security.

SOL: You talk about the nonlearning situation in our schools. How do you apply this to the advanced sciences such as medicine, neurological surgery—some of these things which are tremendously intricate and tremendously advanced, at least from the point of view of the typical medical scientist?

LEARY: Which requires training—

SOL: Right, which requires, in fact, maybe a systemized, formalized training institution.

LEARY: No, no. I don't go along with that at all. It is true that more and more of the professions require long, disciplined periods of training. I'm not advocating the return to some romantic life of savagery. We can't do away with modern science. It's here to stay, and it's going to continue to develop. I'm simply against the mass impersonal granting of thousands of Ph.D.'s in physics to men who never really experienced energy inside their own body, but simply memorize canned equations. Such anthill mentalities, no matter how clever they are at engineering, are going to develop bombs or faster and faster robot vehicles and are going to take man further and further away from his ultimate being, his living, organic nature. Knowledge doesn't depend upon these huge public-supported mind machines that we now call universities. In particular, the State of California is much more susceptible to this type of impersonal "learning" factory.

SoL: Now we've covered the drop-out phase of your slogan—

Leary: I'd like to say more about the drop-out. People think when we say drop-out, we mean become just a lazy, idle person; just take LSD and contemplate the beauty of your navel. The facts are that dropping out is hard work; dropping out requires courage; dropping out releases your energy so that you turn on and release energies. What are you going to do with these energies? Are you going to go back to Valley State College and learn how to be a Ph.D. robot? You drop out of the fake-television American game to find a way of harnessing the energies you are releasing. The people here at Millbrook are full of energy, as you have noticed as you move around the house. They're extremely healthy and they're very hard-working. It takes a considerable amount of energy to convert a sort of jungle like this place to a place of harmony and beauty. You drop out to free your energies for high-level functioning. By drop out, we don't mean fall out; if you want to fall out, be a nice conforming robot and stay in college, and you just drift along the addictive path of middle-class success—that's the easy way.

SoL: Would you care to comment upon the "turn on" phase of your slogan?

Leary: Well, it's been known for thousands of years that man can change consciousness and the levels of energy and wisdom inside, or what is sometimes called revelation—that is, direct

personal experience. In every culture there have been men who
have studied consciousness. They have been called shamans or
gurus or alchemists. These men have studied the science of
expanding consciousness. Most people don't realize that consciousness expansion is as equally complex a problem as the
study of physics, because the nervous system and the levels of
consciousness available to man are infinite in their complexities.
And the techniques and methods of turning on and controlling
the flow and energies of awareness and of mapping where you
have gone and of helping others to make these explorations is
very similar to the use of the microscope, because the microscope turns you on to levels of energy which are invisible to the
naked eye. Turning on requires a change in the physiology of
the human body. You can't turn yourself on with your mind;
you can't turn yourself on with work. You have to have something to bring about the biochemical change; it's called a
sacrament. Today we turn on with chemicals because we live in
a chemical society. In 10 or 15 years, chemicals such as LSD will
be outmoded. We will be using electronic and electrical methods of expanding consciousness because like it or not, consciousness is a biochemical electrical network, and the way to trigger
this off and use it to its fullest extent is through chemical
electrical technique.

SOL: Would you care to . . . You mentioned that through
thousands of years, man has sought ways to turn on. What
various ways have there been other than the current LSD
method? I think we're all familiar with peyote.

LEARY: Well, we mustn't just think of LSD. There are 80-
some known substances in the United States today that can give
you the psychedelic effect. There are new chemicals that are
being developed in our alchemy laboratories each month. I
heard recently of 32 new compounds which are ready to be
released when it is appropriate to do so. All these are legal, and
they don't even exist in any of the statutes; they don't even exist
in the patent office. But in addition to the chemical means of
turning on, there are many nondrug methods which all eventually involve the way the dervishes do in the Middle East.

SOL: Do you feel that in this same interpretation or same meaning, the dances that teen-agers do today and for the past several thousand years are a form of turning on and are not viewed in this perspective?

LEARY: Well, the dance was originally a psychedelic way of expressing one's self, a way of getting high. Unfortunately, most of these early sacramental methods get worn out and routinized so that the Catholic goes to mass today, follows through a series of routine steps, failing to realize that the Catholic mass is an incredibly powerful psychedelic trip, involving transubstantiation of energy, involving a death-birth sequence, and using all sorts of sensory techniques: incense, genuflection, posture, and so forth.

SOL: Do you feel that there is a potential religion in the dance?

LEARY: I think most of the dances that Americans do today don't get them high. They tend to be stylized fads: the monkey, the slop, the twist, the watusi, and so forth. We are trying to get young people to develop dances which are spiritual. We have Bali Ram, the great Indian dancer, living here. He's teaching us how body movements can get you grooving with your internal energies instead of doing the mash potato and the whip. The movements can be in tune with your ancient cellular-mythic patterns, and the dance itself can be a wild ecstatic turn-on spiritual event.

SOL: "Tune in" is the last part of the slogan which you have, and by this do you mean more than just the turning on . . . do you intend direction?

LEARY: Yes, "tune in" means you take the energies you release when you turn on and you come back to the world and you tune these energies in, you harness them, you express your reactions, reverie, and revelations in works of beauty. The tuning-in process is dropping back in and changing your life, changing the way you dress, changing the way you look, changing the place where you live, changing the sequence of your activities. So that increasingly, every act becomes sanctified. All actions are part of a sacred sequence—eating, making a living—

instead of being robot work all these activities should be tuned in. . . . Hello.

LITTLE GIRL: Hello. Are you taping?

LEARY: Yes, I'm making a tape.

LITTLE GIRL: Oh. Is anything going to come on?

LEARY: No, we're not listening; we're talking, we're making the tape. Then we'll listen to it later, and we'll laugh at ourselves. How wise and pompous and smug we are.

LITTLE GIRL: I wanna say something in that.

LEARY: All right, why don't you say something?

LITTLE GIRL: Hello, Timothy!

LEARY: Hello, Kathy.

LITTLE GIRL: I love you, Timothy!!

LEARY: I love you, Kathy.

SOL: The tune-in phase of the slogan of the key or guide, I think, is something that is probably misunderstood by most people. It's the idea that the person who goes on a psychedelic kick is dropping into an unstructured, unmoving, valueless state of affairs from which there will be no continuation of human progress or human development. Would you explain how you would counter these charges?

LEARY: Yes, because the average American thinks that taking a drug makes you drunk. The average American thinks of getting high as going to a cocktail party because booze is our national sacrament. Now alcohol is a "down" experience. It narrows consciousness and makes you rather sloppy, a rather messy person in thought and action. The psychedelic drugs will take you in the opposite direction. They bring you into levels of reality which aren't structured because your mind can't structure them. But the panoramas and the levels that you get into with LSD are exactly those areas which men have called the confrontation of God. The LSD trip is the classic visionary-mystic voyage. I warn everyone not to take LSD unless they're prepared to have all their certainties and social securities shattered. You can't take LSD and come back to the television studios at San Fernando Valley State College and play that out with the same enthusiasm. You just can't pick up your robot role again. This means that psychedelic people act differently for the most part when they come back. But they act; they're not just sitting around passively. In the last 6 or 7 years a small group of us, which has grown with almost miraculous rapidity, has brought about a change in the consciousness of the United States. Now we've done this through action and through effective action and through tuned-in action. Lazy, confused, disorganized people don't bring about this sort of revolution in consciousness that we've brought about in this country. However, the sort of action we recommend throws terror into the hearts of the people who direct the television studio in Sacramento or in Washington or in the administration offices of San Fernando Valley State College. Because the kids that come back from these trips just won't buy the middle-aged menopausal mind system.

SOL: Would you care to elaborate on the phrase "menopausal mind"?

LEARY: Yes. I say there's one word which explains politics, economics and social conflict today. It's not "left" or "right"— it's "age." The men who are running your college and your state and your government had their minds frozen somewhere between 1914 and 1920. That's when their vision of God and the world was formed, and baby, they're not going to change it. It's frozen in a World War I–Depression mentality, and we are now in a social process that is a thousand years beyond what they knew in high school and college. If you study the political events of the last two elections, you'll see that this age variable predicted some of the election surprises. Whenever you had a young, virile man whose eyes looked alive and looked as though he was carrying seed and who looked as though he could make love, he almost invariably defeated the older candidate regardless of how liberal the older candidate's words might have sounded. I think we have an ominous situation in the United States today because of this menopausal mentality. The reason we have this insane political setup in the world today is because of these impotent and senile duffers, Mao in China, De Gaulle in France, Johnson here, playing out their visions of 40, 50, and

60 years ago and very eager to send young, seed-carrying men to carry out their chess games of status and prestige. If everyone just took six months or one year and just dropped out, the creaky menopausal structure of the American power will just slowly crumble. I think every teen-age and college kid should go home and turn on their mother and father. "Come, Father, take off your shoes, feel the sand in your feet. Come on, Grandma, and light up, enjoy the beauties of nature around you."

SOL: By "turn on," did you mean psychedelically turn on or enlighten otherwise?

LEARY: Turn them on in any way that you can. To turn on means to come to your senses. Older people start losing the internal power; they lose that connection of the 2-million-year thread of life and they get frightened and they want to have metal around them. The grandmother wants to have a metal kitchen, she wants to have a metal car, she wants to have steel around the country. This is a psychology of fear, fear of death and the fear of the loss of vigor. The kids should go home and turn on their parents by bringing her flowers and by bringing them music and by urging them to enjoy life. I think, for instance, that Johnson should go down and lie in the sun with Adam Clayton Powell, and he should come back to his senses and learn how to make love again. People who are carrying seed are concerned with the perpetuation of seed. It isn't conceivable to me that a young man or woman of twenty-five would do anything to blow up this planet. Though the men of fifty or sixty who are only going to be around for 10 or 15 years, sure, why, they would gladly blow the thing up for some concept of status and prestige.

SOL: Why then, from the way you talk, I think we have jumped over some previous and necessary philosophical analyzation. What, to you, is the most basic, important, and essential point of life? I assume from the way you speak that it is the carrying of the seed, the regeneration of life itself through life and that this should be the central focal point of our lives, instead of such things as power, national honor and things of this sort. What should be the centering element of the energy forces?

LEARY: Well, you've given me the answer to the question. Centering and harmony is the seed concept of all energy and of all life. Tolkien said in his wonderful trilogy *The Fellowship of the Ring*, where you had the forces of metal, fire and power opposed to the people who want to live in harmony with nature and to live free. Freedom and harmony are the keys to our religion and to the political movement to where it evolved in the United States today. Freedom to find your own inner potentiality and to develop it without coercion from an external centralized authoritarian political entity. To get back in harmony with your own body and with life around you. Modern American man is completely out of rhythm with nature; he is out of rhythm with the seasons; he is out of rhythm with the planets; he is out of rhythm with the soil. In the political situation there is going to be, in my opinion, a spiritual regeneration which is going to be brought about by turning on yourself and finding the basic rhythm inside and then turning it back in.

SOL: I would like to talk for a second about the alleged harmful effects of LSD to people biologically, physiologically and also some of the purported good effects it can have upon people. Do you care, first of all, to explain some of the good effects that you think it has had socially or that it can have socially?

LEARY: You seem to equate good with social good. We feel you can't do good unless you feel good. You can't have a good society unless you have individuals who are turned on and are tuning in.

SOL: The specific answer to which I was pointing to earlier was, is there any indication that persons who are or have been narcotic have been helped out of their addiction with LSD?

LEARY: I can introduce you to five of them right on this property, today.

SOL: Is there or has there been any indication that persons who have had sexual hang-ups such as homosexuality, or monosexuality, if you would, can be helped out of this hang-up through LSD?

LEARY: Yes, there have been many studies which have supported this that we know to be true personally. The psychedelic experience can help a person get back into a harmonious sexual activity. Homosexuality, for the most part, is a psychological or learned distortion. Since man is basically the seed-carrying male, he'll realize that he's been designed by the genetic code to act as the man and to pass on seed in the male way, so LSD may act as a specific aid to homosexuality. But only if the homosexual wants to change; there is no panacea here.

SOL: You feel that there is needed research in this area? Or to your knowledge, is there any research being carried on in this area?

LEARY: Let me say something about research. The term *research* is the biggest sacred cow we got going in our country today. It is 99 percent phony. Any time you hear someone say he is going to do research, watch out because he is likely to be intruding upon your privacy for his own profit. We have no interest in doing research on LSD. Doing research on consciousness is very much like doing research on sex. Occasionally some psychiatrist wants to hook up a couple that he can persuade to perform sexual activities in the laboratory to study heart palpitations and temperature during lovemaking. If people want to do that, it is all right. But you know and I know that research on sex has to be done by you yourself. One of the problems of LSD in the United States today is that psychiatrists have tried to do research on LSD and have gotten nowhere, or they simply haven't had the experience themselves. Their interpretation and explanation of the LSD effect is exactly the interpretation of someone who hasn't had any sexual experience. Suppose some psychiatrist who had never had any sexual experience were to get a couple, and he would hook them up with tachometers and blood-pressure instruments and EKG and give them psychological tests during intercourse, and you see what a picture he paints! "Why, the simple task of performing multiplication and division is lost during sexual intercourse! [*Laughter*] Blood pressure goes up! . . . You froth at the mouth! . . . You utter strange animal cries! . . . Why, they're hardly civilized human beings! . . . They thrash around and knock vases off the tables! . . . They wouldn't talk to you in a sensible way! . . . They wouldn't talk about rational things like Nixon versus Reagan! Clearly this is a dangerous, convulsive type of experience, both psychologically and socially, which should be banned!" There have been plenty who would say exactly that about the sexual experience. If you give LSD to someone and he sits there quietly and won't talk to you for three hours, you say, "Oh, he's in a catatonic stupor," but then you talk to him later, and he says, "Stupor? No, I was flipping through revelations and delights of ecstasy. I was more alive than I'd ever been in my life." We're very much against the taboo of sacred cow research. You've got to do the research on your own consciousness. YOU've got to do the research on your own intimate way of life. No Big Brother daddy with an M.D. or Ph.D. can do these things for you. It's this Western engineering technological notion that people can do things for other people with forms of energy.

SOL: What about the rumors of chromosomal disorders that have popped up lately?

LEARY: Well, now we'll get to your second question that has to deal with the dangers, but let me say one thing about the benefits of LSD. LSD is a key to releasing energy. Like any form of energy, it can be misused in the hands of the reckless or in the hands of the foolish, or in the hands of people who want to exploit for their own power motives. The real misuse of LSD is when it's in the hands of someone who would do it to someone else. The only control of LSD is self-control. The only benefits of LSD are the benefits you are willing to discipline yourself to get. You get from an LSD experience only what you bring to it and what you're ready to take away from it. There's a real panacea here. The benefits of LSD get you involved in the most difficult, disciplined yoga of all, 'cause you're learning how to use your head and learning how to use your body. Now the harms and dangers of LSD are mainly its danger to society. There's no evidence yet that LSD brings about any physiological damage. There's no evidence yet that LSD has any effect upon the brain itself in a deleterious way. Now it may, in the future, turn out to have effects we don't understand yet. Anyone who takes LSD is gambling; it's a risk. Of course, everything in our society is a risk. Putting your nervous system in front of a television tube and being battered by all those radiations may bring about changes that we don't understand. Now as far as the chromosomal or genetic changes brought about by LSD, there was one research done at Buffalo which was a straight out-and-out hoax, and subsequent studies of this sort will demonstrate that this was a political piece of research designed admittedly before the research was done to prove that it was dangerous. It was done by a man named Cohen. These studies were in vetro—that means cells that were in tubes, not in the living organism. Changes in those cells could be brought about by any number of substances in the heavy dosages they were using, and it tells nothing about any changes. There's no evidence from these anthropological sources or from the clinical data provided by the hundreds of LSD babies that are being born each year that would suggest danger. . . . There are LSD babies right around this house. They were conceived under LSD and born during LSD experiences.

SOL: You were saying that through thousands of years of usage there is no evidence that hallucinogens have affected our evolutionary code?

LEARY: No, there are specific tribes in Mexico, the Maztec tribe, which uses psilocybin, and I know of no evidence that any harmful mutations have taken place.

SOL: What form of—?

LEARY: On the other hand, I want to make it clear that I'm not saying anything positive about LSD. I'm not saying in this interview that anyone automatically benefits from LSD, and serious questions are raised in our minds all the time about the use of LSD. How much energy and neurological revelation can the frenzied human mind tolerate without flipping out? LSD possibly shouldn't be used in the widespread way in which it is. We seriously concern ourselves about such questions. But we do object to pseudoscientific statements from psychiatrists and public health officials which breed fear and panic in the American people about scientific questions that won't be answered for decades.

SOL: What form of society do you envision 50 years from today?

LEARY: We have worked out very detailed blueprints, prophecies and predictions as to what we think will happen in the next 50, the next 100, even the next 500 years. But I hesitate to attempt to spell this out now because it sounds too farfetched; it would sound like science fiction, speculation. The profession of the prophet, and anyone who takes LSD is likely to be thrown into this profession, is a very risky one because we see things that can happen, and we have to be careful how much information we feed back to our primitive social system before they think we are nuts, before they blame us for what is inevitably going to happen. We predicted 6 years ago that there was going to be a psychedelic revolution; now they listen to us. We went to Washington and told the FDA that this was going to happen.

Now, when it happened, when millions of kids started turning on, Caesar and his bureaucrats blamed us for the psychedelic inundation. But to go back to your question, with all these preliminary qualifications, man is going to get back in harmony with his body, with fellow man, and with other forms of life on this planet. Man is going to realize that consciousness is the key to human life, and instead of power struggles over territory and possession of weapons, the focus of man's energies is going to be on consciousness. Pierre Teilhard de Chardin, the great Jesuit philosopher, has spelled out the psychedelic vision in which the world will become unified in one field of consciousness. This will happen through the mass media in the hands of individuals, not networks. It will also happen through the psychedelic experience. The differences which cause conflicts among men and between man and other forms of nature are going to be brought back in harmony. All metal, concrete, electricity and atomic energy is going to go underground. Man is going to realize that his precarious hold on this strange planet depends upon a thin film of about 10 inches of topsoil, and it's a very delicate balance of energies of cellular and different species that

keeps his delicate web of life going. Every time man takes metal
or stone from under the ground and puts it in sheets over the
delicate, sensitive skin of the planet, he is killing and disrupting
this net. So you will find all technology underground. The city
of New York 200 years from now will look as it did 200 years
ago. The air will recapture the life-giving balance it is supposed
to have. The rivers and waters will not be polluted. Man is
going to tidy up the mess he's made in this very recent technological fling. Man has just been intoxicated by machines for 200
years. He is going to come off it and sober up. Man is also going
to discover that machines are no fun. That fun comes from the
senses and from your body and from human interaction and
consciousness. Everything is centered on consciousness, and no
amount of steel and metal and apparatus is going to give one
second of real ecstasy or real communion.

SOL: Where will the people live when this type of a parklike
atmosphere or a natural state has returned to the earth?

LEARY: People will live some of the time under the ground
and some of the time above the ground in buildings which will
be harmonized with the soil and plant life around them. Now
this will sound like science fiction or fantasy, but actually we are
doing this at Millbrook, and if you look around at this property
you will see an embryonic stage of these wild predictions going
on. We even have soil on the roof to symbolize to us that this is
a cave we live in, this house. And you will find if you go out
into the woods today, members of our community building little
cottages and tepees, who want to live out in the woods this
summer. You will see in our meditation gardens and in our
daily activities here a slow cellular development toward this
utopia which I have been describing. We think that our prophecies and our scientific fantasies are more likely to come true
than any others because if you listen to the government-
supported scientific agencies, they are just predicting to the
next antimissile missile. Most of your politicians are just interested in predicting to the next election. They are interested in
the next intersection of power where their status is going to be
concerned, and there are very few people who are thinking

more than 15 or 20 years ahead. But people who are in tune with their own seed energy, like ourselves, are about the only people who are spinning out blueprints; therefore our blueprint is more likely to come about than the more secular and limited blueprints of the politicians.

SOL: Back just a second to the underground, with the steel and concrete and stuff. H. G. Wells formulated a science fiction story called *The Time Machine,* which predicted a world of this sort back about 20 or 30 years ago. I think he said around the year 2000. He visualized a dualized society where the flower people lived on the surface—

LEARY: Oh, really?

SOL: —and the machine people lived underground. Do you foresee this?

LEARY: Yes. That's interesting. I have not read that nor read those phrases but it is exactly my own conception; it just makes organic sense.

SOL: Have you seen the movie *The Time Machine?*

LEARY: No, I didn't.

SOL: As a matter of fact—

LEARY: I would like to see it.

SOL: —it is parallel to what's happening here.

LEARY: What I think will happen is that man will live aboveground and will recapitulate preseed cycles. Seed cycles where one will relive the entire growth process inside your mother's womb. Then you do it again as you grow up as a child, if you live aboveground; and you will do it again, a third time, if you have children. Now in this society, people will start having children when the DNA thought they should, not when they get their Ph.D. but when they start to become adolescents. The DNA code has designed us to have babies at the age of thirteen, fourteen, fifteen, because that is when the seed power is at its height. But of course, our chessboard, artificial society, postpones this, and it's fighting the wisdom of the DNA code. It is purely possible for someone to have completed the three seed cycles—once in the womb, once growing up yourself, and once growing up with your children—at the age of twenty-three or twenty-four; you are ready to live out of the cycle. I don't think people should be taught control of metal and these potentially antilife energies until they have completed three seed cycles and have enough reverence for, and understanding of life that they can then be allowed to deal with life-killing instruments. The problem is that the person doesn't really—hasn't been turned on to his life seed thing. He thinks nothing of taking these instruments of death into his hands—like the gas engine—and killing life with it. So we have teen-age kids with guns and autos, and this doesn't make sense to our DNA code. At the age of twenty-five or twenty-six you say, well, you have a choice. You can live aboveground, or if you would like to go on to the next level, if you are at that stage of holiness and you understand the sacredness of life, you can be trusted with the more powerful sacraments of electricity and energy. Then you go belowground, and our understanding of the nervous system acceleration, chemically and electronically, is such that you can be taught the symbols of electronic physics. You know, our educational systems are so brutally inefficient and so shamefully disregard the crux of the matter. When we teach kids in school, we teach them not to learn. At the age of twenty, twenty-four, whenever a person is holy enough to learn these more powerful energies, why, then he can learn very quickly. You can teach someone nuclear physics in three or four months. Then he can live underground, he can do his yoga. There will be breakthroughs in physics so that telepathy in 10 or 15 years will be commonplace. Physics is going to expand as more physicists turn on.

SOL: You have mentioned that in keeping with an attunement with the natural stage of our lives, there is a point at which a person should cease to attempt to continue to control or affect things. I want to talk about the menopausal mind and when a person is entering old age. Do you feel at this point that people should just sit back and enjoy life or what there is of it left?

LEARY: Yes, they should realize that the whole thing is a spiritual journey, and the person over fifty, who is dying anyway, who's half dead, should concentrate on coming to terms with his own death and getting an overall perspective and gracefully turning it over to the young people. So we've got to get the older people to turn on. We've got to get big reservations for older people instead of these senior citizens places where we surround them with machines. We've got to get them to do nothing but dance and make love with God. They should radiate humor and mellowness, and they don't care about power anymore, and you should be able to go to older people as you did in the village tribe, and the old man is sitting there barefoot, half-naked, with his beard, and he's glowing, and he doesn't care. A holy man is someone who doesn't care about the little chess game of power; he doesn't care about the chess game of possessions; he doesn't care about sex, even; he's beyond all these bodily things and he's radiating the joys of all of everything. That's why we've got to get our older people to turn on.

Sol: Now I know that it's hard to set arbitrary evaluations, but at that stage, do you feel a person begins to step into this realm that you say ends at around fifty or some stage where the menopausal mind sets in? Where does a person first enter life's power zone, as it were?

Leary: All this has been spelled out in oriental philosophy. The West knows all about machines and fails to realize that all the wisdom has come from the East. The Hindus were dealing with these problems that the psychedelic generation is dealing with 4,000 years ago. It's all spelled out in the sacred teachings of the East, and they say that there are the 4 stages of life in which you've got to learn to use your senses and your seed power, and naturally you're going to enjoy your sensual body. You're going to enjoy making love and to have babies and to support your babies. You're going to have duties, and then you have to have a little power, enough to protect your territory and to feed and support your group. And when your kids are old enough to take over, then you go to the fourth, which is the goal, the end point where you can say, I'm dropping out. I don't have to worry anymore. Now I can just— You go to the holy cities, like Rishikish in India, and there are all these old people there that have been businessmen in Bombay and college professors, and you'll find some old ex-governor Reagans naked in Rishikish going around barefoot, and they've got these orange robes, and it's just a big LSD session. Everyone's high, and you don't care about the British Empire and taxation; they're beyond that. They're just there to hear the roar of the Ganges reminding them that it's been going on for thousands of years.

SOL: Do you anticipate, then, the evolution of a new type of homogeneous society? H. G. Wells' idea was of a polarized society and that they clashed—

LEARY: Yes.

SOL: Do you anticipate a clash now and later the evolution to a homogeneous society, or do you think that the clash will—?

LEARY: The clash can be avoided by consulting your own energy system and seeing that there is a place for everything—a place for the machine people and a place for the seed, flower people; you just have to arrange your own life so that you can follow a harmonious sequence. Now we are very much against polarization. Conflict. There is a danger, though, that it will go that way, there is a danger that man will evolve into different species. We must realize that evolution is not through, that man is not a final product, and just as there are many species of primate, there may be just as many species evolving from what we now call man, *homo sapiens*. It may well be that we'll have two species. One species, which is the machine species, will like to live in metal buildings and skyscrapers and will get their kicks by just becoming part of a machine. That species of man will become an unnecessary, easily worn-out part of the whole technological machinery. In that case, man will become anonymous—just like the anthill or the beehive. Sex will become very depersonalized. It will become very promiscuous. You won't care who you make love to because they're all just replaceable parts. You know, she's the new pretty blond girl who runs the teletype machine, and you'll ball her, and then tomorrow, the secretary who runs the electronic typewriter; so that we may well get a new species who will be technological. But I do know that our seed-flower species will continue. And we may hang out in new pockets of disease which the machine people haven't cleaned up with their antiseptics. And we'll be somewhere out in the marshes, or somewhere out in the woods, laughing at the machine and enjoying our senses and having ecstasies and re-membering where we came from and teaching our children that, believe it or not, we're not machines and we weren't de-signed to make machines and we weren't designed to run ma-chines. I think you have to be a very holy man to appreciate and understand and run a machine because the machine is a beautiful yoga and a beautiful ecstasy. I've nothing against machines; it's just incredible that the DNA code could produce us and then produce these machines. It's part of the glory of God's process, but the machine's got to be seen as a sacrament, not as a god.

SOL: The way our society's structured, currently, legally—un-fortunately, this is the supranatural structure which is imposed upon us—legally a person attains to and reaches the age of ma-turity at the age of twenty-one and continues in that state until his death.

LEARY: Right.

SOL: Now, at what point do you believe a person does attain to this realization of himself?

LEARY: Obey the DNA code! I scoff at the chess-game laws of man; they are all old men that rule and pass such laws. There was never a young teen-ager that passed a law against sex. Right! Or a poor young teen-ager that passed laws about guard-ing a bank. I follow the laws of nature, and nature tells you when someone should vote. Now when a girl menstruates, nature is saying that she is ready, and when a young man reaches puberty, nature is saying that he is ready. One of the terrible things, of course, about the menopausal society is that the older you get, the more brain damaged you are, but in our society, the older you get, the more power you get. So we now have this paradoxical, suicidal situation in the United States, all of the wealth being in the hands of the menopausal people, who are naturally only concerned with protecting this, and that's why we have a very unhappy, violent country. We are physically violent; there is murder, and there's assassination and there is worry. Look at Johnson's face; he is not a happy man. And look at those old devils in Congress; they're not happy, joyous people. It disturbs me as it disturbs all turned-on prophets—there is so much unnecessary suffering. I think that there should be laws that allow people to vote at puberty, and you should certainly take voting away at menopause. No one over the age of fifty should be allowed to vote. Why should they bother? The reason they vote is because they have no trust in the kids, no trust in the seed bearers. If they really trusted the process, they would gladly give up the vote.

SOL: I still have a few questions. Seems like we keep picking up extra ones as we go along: A few moments ago you used the term "God." From your perspective, who, what, where, when, and why is God? [*General laughter*] Because we have concepts of God and so many young, pseudo- or neo-intellectuals become atheistic or nontheistic or pantheistic.

LEARY: A lot of people think I've sold out because we've started a religion. Some kids think that religion means all the hypocrisy of the Congressman, and the faggot minister and the conservative Sunday school and so forth. I think this is tragic—

SOL: Are you using the ploy of religion to get by the LSD laws?

LEARY: No, we had a religion going long before we started our league formally. We were a religious group 5 or 6 years ago, when we originally came here. Like it or not, or believe it or not, I'm convinced that the religious kick is the only experience that makes life worthwhile. The moment of revelation when you're turned on to the whole process, which men of old called the mystic, is the whole purpose of life. The great religious leaders were the greatest figures of all. Buddha was the most turned-on guy. Buddha wanted to get rid of suffering. All the concepts about virtue, hard work, and being good are part of that old con game. Religion to us is ecstasy. It is freedom and harmony. Kids should not let the fake, television-prop religion they were taught as kids turn them off. The real trip is the God trip. Now to get back to the question as to who is God: For thousands of years skeptics have been asking visionaries like me,

"All right, who is God? Does he speak Latin? Does he speak Greek? Does he have a white skin or a black one?" You think I can use a 3,000-word language like English to define a process which is 5 billion years old on this planet and which operates at the speed of light and manifests itself in ever-changing forms? I can teach you how to find God. I can teach you methods; that's my profession. To talk to God yourself, you are going to have to throw away all your definitions and just surrender to this process, and then you can come back and try to tune in and develop an art form which will communicate your vision. God does exist and is to me this energy process; the language of God is the DNA code. Beyond that, the language of God is the nucleus of the atom. Above that, the language of God is the exquisite, carefully worked out dialogue of the planets and the galaxies, etc. And it does exist and there is an intelligence and there is a planfulness and a wisdom and power that you can tune in to. Men have called this process, for the lack of a better word, "God." I know that when I was at Harvard, God was a dirty word; God is "dog" spelled backward. I don't care what you call it. It took me 5 years of taking LSD before I would say the word "God" out loud. Because you have to feel right to say it, and I feel very comfortable now in saying that I do talk to God and I listen to Him. He is a hipster, He is a musician, and He's got a great beat going. You'll never find Him in an institution or in an American television stage set. He's never legal! And He's got a great sense of humor, too! I digressed, and I repeated myself and I don't pretend to talk in any linear fashion. I'm not writing a book or a paragraph. I'm more like a musician, and I repeat riffs. . . . You can feel free to edit, cut out, or move it around any way that you want. I hope you will, for I've been repeating myself.

SOL: One last question. It is necessary, you said, to protect property rights. It will be necessary for there to be some basic rules.

LEARY: Render unto Caesar everything external.

SOL: What is Caesar?

LEARY: Society, politics, rules.

SOL: How would this be achieved in the projected society which could be achieved, ideally? Would we have to elect 1 out of every 15 persons and have him go and represent those 15? Will there be tribal elders?

LEARY: Democracy is a failure because it is based upon a political unit which is not organic—the individual mind. The political unit should be the tribe; property should be held by the tribe, by the extended family. Voting should be by the extended family. The idea that one man decides to vote for Johnson or Goldwater. Ha, ha! Some choice, right? My mind is going to decide. That's putting too much burden on my mind; it exaggerates my personality. We must return to—advance to— the tribal unit of society.

SEAL OF THE LEAGUE

4

God's Secret Agent A.O.S.3*

Rosemary and I had been waiting for Him for five hours. He's always and deliberately erratic about appointments. Science fiction James Bond paranoia. Throw off police surveillance. Suddenly I could feel His presence. A telepathic hit. He really does emit powerful vibrations. A minute later His boots drummed on the walk.

He looked tired, pale, but the furry, quick animal tension was still there. Black leather sleeveless jacket. Wide-sleeved, multicolored theatrical shirt. Jangling bells. The magician. The electronic wizard.

He had been up several days working in his laboratory and was coming off an acid high. He wanted to be warm.

Rosemary and I built up the fire, lit candles and fell out on a low divan. He paced the floor in front of us. He's not tall, and He likes to stay above His listeners, higher than everyone else, moving while they rest.

He started a three-hour rap about energy, electronics, drugs, politics, the nature of God and the place of man in the divine system. Laughing at His own brilliance, turning himself on, turning us on. Einsteinian physics and Buddhist philosophy translated into the fast, right, straight rhythm of acid-rock hip.

The television folk heroes of today are the merry outlaws of the past. The television Robin Hoods of the future, the folk heroes of the twenty-first century, will be the psychedelic drug

---

* He doesn't want me to use his name.

promoters of the 1960's. A good bet for romantic immortality is
A.O.S.3. God's Secret Agent A.O.S.3, acid king, LSD millionaire,
test-tube Pancho Villa, is the best-known of a band of dedicated,
starry-eyed chemical crusaders who outwitted the wicked, gun-
toting federals and bravely turned on the land of the young and
the free to the electronic harmony of the future.

In the daily press the Reagans and Romneys merit the
adulatory headlines. The Holy Alchemists, if mentioned at all,
are denounced as sordid criminals. But the simple truth is that
the Reagans and Romneys will soon be forgotten. Can anyone
remember which Republicans were struggling for the nomina-
tion in 1956?

The mythic folk heroes of our times will be the psychedelic-
drug outlaws, the science fiction Johnny Appleseeds who build
secret laboratories, scrounge the basic chemicals, experiment,
experiment, experiment to develop new ecstasy pills, who test
their homemade sacraments on their own bodies and the flesh of
their trusting friends, who distribute the precious new waters of
life through a network of dedicated colleagues, forever underground, hidden, as the mysteries have always been hidden from
the hard-eyed agents of Caesar, Pharaoh, Herod, Pope Paul,
Napoleon, Stalin, Lyndon B. Nixon and J. Edgar Hoover.

For the last seven years I have watched with admiration these
LSD frontiersmen, the Golden Bootleggers, manufacture and
pass on the sacraments. Laughing, pupil-dilated, visionary alchemists who seek nothing less than the sudden mind-blowing
liberation of their fellow man.

First, of course, there was reluctant Albert Hoffman of
Sandoz, the staid, involuntary agent mysteriously selected to
give LSD to the human race. The full story of this remarkable
Swiss scientist remains to be told. But this much I have heard.
His first LSD trips were deep, revelatory religious experiences.
The establishment press tries to tell us that Hoffman's first
sessions were accidental and frightening and freaky. The facts
are that Hoffman, a spiritual man, grasped immediately the
implications of his discovery and initiated a high-level, ethical,
gentleman's conspiracy of philosophically minded scientists to

disseminate LSD for the benefit of the human race. His tactical mistake (if, indeed, he made one) was to work through the established professions, failing to see that a complete revision of social form would necessarily follow the use of his discovery.

Rosemary had made tea and put a red sanctuary light on the gold-framed madonna. He paced in front of us like a newly caged animal. (Rosemary, what kind of animal is He? Oh, He's furry, warm, nervous, whiskers twitching, ears alert, carnivorous but gentle. Like a squirrel, but bigger. Perhaps a badger or a raccoon. They are very intelligent.)

He preaches: Oh, man, how beautifully it all fits together. Dig, the first atomic fission occurred in December 1942.

Is that the one in the Chicago squash court?

Yeah. Now dig. The Van Allen belt is a thick blanket of electronic activity protecting this planet. What is the earth? A core of molten metals covered by a thin layer of soft, vulnerable, organic tissue. Life nibbling away, nibbling away at the rock beneath. All life on this planet is a delicate network unified. Each living form feeding on the others. And being eaten. The Van Allen belt is the higher intelligence protecting earth from lethal solar radiation, and it's in touch with every form of living intelligence on the earth—vegetable, animal, human.

I laughed. Alchemist, you are so orthodox! Our Father who art in heaven above! I pointed upward. He really is up there, huh? Thy kingdom come, thy will be done on earth as it is in the Van Allen belt!

He didn't stop to acknowledge my comment. Somehow He records neurologically what I say and reprograms it, and prints it back out to me in endless tapes of electronic poety, but He never listens.

Now dig. The Supreme Intelligence sees that man has rediscovered atomic energy. Wow! We gotta stop those cats before they disrupt the whole living network. The only thing DNA fears is radiation. That's why the Van Allen belt is there.

OK, now get this. Four months after the first fission, Hoffman accidentally, ha ha, rediscovers LSD, which is now psychoactive.

Rediscovers?

Yeah, man. Actually Hoffman first synthesized LSD in 1938, but it gave no hit. No turn-on. Now why is it that Hoffman handles LSD in 1938 and nothing happens and then in 1943, three months after atomic energy is released, he puts his finger on lysergic acid and gets flipped out? What happened? Did Hoffman suddenly get careless? Or had LSD suddenly been changed into a psychedelic chemical? Competent chemists just don't change their handling of compounds. Hoffman's techniques are standard.

His eyes are dancing and He's laughing and his hands and body are moving. He was a ballet dancer once before He started making drugs.

Now dig. The atomic fission in December 1942 changed the whole system of energy in this solar system. The higher intelligence decides to make a few simple changes in the electronic structure of some atoms, and zap! We have LSD, an incredibly powerful substance that is the exact antidote to atomic energy. People take LSD, and flash! They get the message and start putting things back in harmony with the great design. Stop war! Wear flowers! Conservation! Turning on people to LSD is the precise and only way to keep war from blowing up the whole system.

Hoffman's plan was to persuade square psychiatrists and medical researchers to use LSD. But of course, it never happens that way. The respectable researchers were afraid. They didn't get the point. So the first far-out, messianic apostle-alchemist of the psychedelic age was a rum-drinking, snake-oil-fundamentalist-Bible Belt salesman type named Hal Lubbard. Like A.O.S.3, Hal Lubbard is a legendary, behind-the-scenes operator whose brilliance was deliberatly shielded behind a veil of rumor. This much is known. In the 1950's Lubbard was turned on to LSD and got the message at once. He had made money in uranium mining during the forties and saw the connection right away. (Do you?) Then this incredible shaman playing the role of an uneducated, coarse, blustering, Roman Catholic hillbilly boozer proceeded to turn on several dozen top sophisticated scientists and show them the sacramental meaning of LSD.

When the medical associations complained about nonmedics dispensing drugs, Hal chuckled and bought a doctor's degree from a diploma store in the South for fifty dollars, and as Doctor-Tongue-in-Cheek, Lubbard was accepted admiringly by psychiatrist Osmond, scientist Hofer, and Aldous Huxley and philosopher Gerald Heard and even Sidney Cohen of UCLA. Hal Lubbard was the first psychedelic tactician to see that supply-control of the drug would be a key issue in the future, so he kept up a mysterious schedule of procurement-distribution flights. East Coast–West Coast–East Europe–West Europe, bargaining, wheedling, swapping to build up the first underground supply of the most precious substance the world has ever known. The current retail price of LSD is from $20,000 to $50,000 a gram. A million dollars an ounce.

Lubbard's plan was to have a chain of medically approved LSD clinics throughout the country. It was a brilliant, utopian, American-businessman stroke of genius and would have, among other things, ended the threat of war on this planet, but Lubbard failed to realize that spiritual revelations and Buddhist ecstasies were the last thing that the medical associations and government bureaus run by J. Edgar Lyndon were going to approve, and the International Foundation for Advanced Studies, his pilot clinic in Menlo Park, California (which turned on several hundred of the most influential people in the San Francisco Bay area), was ruthlessly closed by the FDA in spite of its impressive psychiatric and medical credentials. So Hal Lubbard dropped out, disappeared and was reincarnated in the new form of Dr. Spaulding.

It was a gray, cold, winter day in 1962. Dick Alpert and I took the day off from Harvard and flew in Dick's plane to New York. Dick's father was president of the New Haven Railroad, and the cop under Grand Central saluted as we got into the huge black Cadillac with the license plate NHRR, which was equipped with two-way radio and an extra set of wheels to run on tracks.

I asked Dick, "Who owns Grand Central Station?"

He said, "Pennsylvania Railroad owns half, and we own half."

*Dick was good at throwing away lines. We headed south to visit
a chemical factory. Going through the waterfront-Mafia section
of Jersey City, I had to laugh. Two Harvard professors driving
in a black limousine through the dark slum city to score drugs
which would change the world.*

*In the wood-paneled conference room of Sandoz Laboratories
the top pharmaceutical executives laughed uneasily. We are a
medical drug house. How can we market an ecstasy pill to be
used by God seekers? The vice-president grinned. Let's say LSD
isn't a drug. Let's call it a food and bottle it like Coca-Cola! The
company lawyer's reflex frown. As a food, it still must be
licensed by the FDA, and they think medical.*

*The conference was a failure. They were sympathetic but
weren't going to lose their AMA-FDA respectability by releasing LSD to the public. We shook hands, and Dick said, "Well,
gentlemen, we'll have to do your marketing for you." And we
all laughed.*

*One of the crew-cut executives escorted us down to the car.
On the elevator, he suddenly pulled a pill bottle out of his
pocket and shoved it in my hand. "I've taken LSD. I know
what's happening. Here's five grams. Don't say where you got it.
Use it wisely."*

By this time (1962) we had set up a loose but effective distribution system for free LSD. A university psychologist in the
Midwest. A God-intoxicated businessman in Atlanta. A few
God-loving ministers and rabbis. David Soloman, at that time
editor of the jazz magazine *Metronome*. Allen Ginsberg. Dozens
of holy psychiatrists. All giving psychedelics to people they
knew were ready for the trip. A responsible network of friends.

Every time our supplies would run low, a new shaman-
alchemist would appear.

Like Bernie and Barnie, the flipped-out desert holy men, who
had been taking the peyote trip with the Indians for years and
writing crazy, brilliant, illiterate books on telepathy and accelerated learning through LSD. Bernie claimed to have mastered
the German language in two acid sessions. They had learned
how to make LSD, which they distributed in rubber-stopped

bottles, a strange brown elixir with curious green seaweed strands. They sold the sacrament at bargain rates to dozens of famous people in California before they were treacherously betrayed to the feds. They didn't get along well with their defense attorneys and built their case around an insane plot to get the judge and jury to taste their brew, which would have revolutionized jurisprudence forever. But the judge recoiled in horror and gave them 19-year sentences, which they jumped. God be with you, beloved guides, wherever you are.

Some time later (the exact date must be kept vague) I was lecturing in a college town. A note to my hotel. Please call a Doctor Spaulding. Urgent. Had to see me after the lecture.

He was a distinguished-looking man in his fifties. One of the ten leading chemists in the country. Big-boned, handsome, jolly, athlete-scholar type.

He drove his car with strange jungle caution, checking the rear-view mirror, doubling around blocks. He drove to the middle of a deserted supermarket parking lot and stopped the car. Cloak and dagger. He came right to the point. He had taken LSD several times. He knew what it would do. He also knew that the government was alarmed. A lot of high-level people had turned on and knew that LSD was a religious experience. But they were worried. Big power struggle over control of drugs in Washington. The narcotics bureau of the Treasury Department wanted to keep all drugs illegal, to step up law enforcement, add thousands of T-men, G-men and narks to the payroll. On the other hand, the medics and scientists in the government wanted the FDA to handle all drugs, including heroin, pot, LSD. Make it a medical matter. Would I make a deal? Would I tell the FDA all I knew about the black market and smash the underground distribution of LSD? If I cooperated, I'd be guaranteed research approval to use LSD. We had to help the FDA get control of the drugs. Then marijuana and LSD would be legal for licensed use. But we had to keep the kids from getting LSD or the hard-line-cop faction in Washington would get the anti-LSD legislation they wanted. If I didn't cooperate, I'd be busted.

I looked at him and laughed. Not a chance. This is a country
of free citizens. LSD and marijuana are none of the government's business to give or take away. If it's a choice, I'd rather
have the kids using LSD than the doctors. Kids are holier. And
if it's a choice between becoming a government informer or get
busted, I'll go to jail.

Dr. Spaulding laughed knowingly. Okay, I had to make the
offer, but I knew you wouldn't scare. But you should know that
a big government crackdown is coming. All the sources of LSD
will be sealed off. You better stock up. How much do you have
on hand now?

Not much. A few thousand doses.

How much LSD can you use?

I looked at him in surprise. He starts out like a fed, and now
he's offering me acid.

He saw my look and started to explain. A few of us saw this
coming several years ago. We started stockpiling the raw lysergic acid base. We have the largest supply of LSD in the world.
More than Sandoz, more than Red China, more than our Defense Department. We want to give it away to responsible
people who won't try to profit by it and who can get it out to
the people. Okay. How much can you distribute in one year?

The scene was surrealistic. This famous, eminently respectable professor offering to set us up with unlimited supplies of
acid. It was hard to keep from laughing. I asked him one question—why?

Oh, you know why, Tim. Can you see any hope for this
homicidal, neurologically crippled species other than a mass
religious ecstatic convulsion? Okay. How much do you want?

We can get rid of 200 grams in a year. That's 2 million
doses.

Dr. Spaulding nodded. Fine. You'll receive a four-year supply—a thousand grams in the next few weeks. Each package will
contain 100 grams of LSD powder. Get scales to put it in doses.
Keep it sterile. Alcohol or even vodka. Dilute it down. If you
can't get a pill machine, dilute it down and drop it on sugar
cubes.

He started the car and drove back to my hotel. How many people are you distributing to this way? Not many, he answered. In chemistry, every process has to develop at its own natural tempo. We have enough LSD stored now to keep every living American turned on for several years.

That was the only time I met Dr. Spaulding. A week later the acid began arriving at Millbrook—in brown manila envelopes and hollowed-out books mailed from different cities throughout the country. In hardly any time at all we had given away 10 million doses.

It was ten in the evening by now. Rosemary and I were starved. A.O.S.3 was still too high to be hungry, but He was responding telepathically to our stomach pangs. Organic matter nibbling the granite, each life form eating each other. Endless transformation of energy. Galaxies feeding each other.

Alchemist, do us a favor and don't mention eating, okay? We haven't had supper yet.

He was spinning us along an epic-poem trip through the levels of creation. He can really tell it. I've studied with the wisest sages of our times—Huxley, Heard, Lama Govinda, Sri Krishna Prem, Alan Watts—and I have to say that A.O.S.3, college flunk-out, who never wrote anything better (or worse) than a few rubber checks, has the best up-to-date perspective of the divine design I've ever listened to.

To begin with, He begins where they all begin—at the beginning. He had taken the full LSD trip, hurled down through His cellular reincarnations, disintegrated beyond life into pulsing electron grids, whirled down beyond atomic form to that unitary center that is one, pure, radiant humming vibration. Yin. Yin. Yin. Yang. Yang. Yang.

His face was glowing, and He was screaming that full-throated God cry that was torn from the lungs of Moses and shrieked by San Juan de la Cruz and which Rosemary and I heard most recently just after our sunrise wedding on the desert mountain top bellowed by the bone-tissue-blood trumpet of Ted Marckland—the eternal, unmistakable cry of the man who has heard God's voice and shouted back in joyous, insane acceptance. If

*you've ever opened your ears to anyone who has surrendered,
wide-eyed, to the sound of God, you know what I mean.*

*He shook his head and laughed. I can't say it in words. God,
man, I've got to learn a musical instrument so I can really say
what it sounds like.*

*Yes, A.O.S.3 carries the official stamp on His skin's passport
that He has been where all the great mystics have been—that
point where you see it all and hear it all and know it all belongs
together. But how can you describe an electronic rhythm of
which 5 billion years of our planetary evolution is just one beat?
He is in the same position as every returned visionary—grab-
bing at ineffective words. But check His prophetic credentials.
High native intelligence coupled with a photographic memory.
Solid grasp of electronics. Absorbed biological texts. Knows
computer theory. Has hung out with the world's top orientalists
and Hindu scholars. Has lived with and designed amplifiers for
the farthest-out rock band, the Dateful Gread. As a sniffing,
alert, inquisitive mammal of the twentieth century, He has
poked His quivering, whiskered nose into all the dialects and
systems by which man attempts to explain the divine.*

Throughout history the alchemist has always been a magical,
awesome figure. The potion. The elixir. The secret formulary.
Experimental metaphysics. Those old alchemists weren't really
trying to transmute lead to gold. That's just what they told the
federal agents. They were actually looking for the philosopher's
stone. The waters of life. The herb, root, vine, seed, fruit,
powder that would turn on, tune in and drop out.

And every generation or so, someone would rediscover the
key. And the key is always chemical. Consciousness is a chemical
process. Learning, sensing, remembering, forgetting are altera-
tions in a biochemical book. Life is chemical. Matter is chemical.

*His bells jingling as He gesticulates. Everything is hooked
together with electrons. And if you study how electrons work,
you learn how everything is hooked up. You are close to God.
Chemistry is applied theology.*

The alchemist-shaman-wizard-medicine man is always a
fringe figure. Never part of the conventional social structure. It

has to be. In order to listen to the shuttling, whispering, ancient language of energy (long faint sighs across the millennia), you have to shut out the noise of the marketplace. You flip yourself out deliberately. Voluntary holy alienation. You can't serve God and Caesar. You just can't.

That's why the wizards who have guided and inspired human destiny by means of revelatory vision have always been socially suspect. Always outside the law. Holy outlaws. Reckless, courageous outlaws. Folklore has it that 43 federal agents were assigned to His case before He was arrested on the day before Christmas, 1967. They have to stop this wild man with jingling bells or He'll turn on the whole world. His Christmas acid could have stopped the war.

Messianic certainty. A.O.S.3 is the most moralistic person I have ever met. Everything is labeled good or bad. Every human activity is either right or wrong. He is, in short, a nagging, preaching, intolerable puritan. Right to Him is what is natural, healthy, harmonious. Right gets you high. Wrong brings you down.

Meat is good. Man is a carnivorous animal, but eat your meat rare.

Vegetables are bad. They are for smoking, not eating. God (or the DNA code) designed ruminants and cud chewers to eat leaves. And man to eat their flesh.

Psychedelic drugs are good.

Alcohol is bad. Unhealthy, dulling, damaging to the brain. A "down" trip. He explains this in ominous chemical warnings. I always feel guilty drinking a beer in front of him.

Showers are good. Clean.

Baths are bad. You soak in your own dirt, and your soft pores sponge up foul debris, in a lukewarm liquid, an ideal nutrient for germs.

Rock 'n' roll is good.

Science fiction is bad. Screws up your head. Takes you on weird trips.

Long hair is good. Sign of a free man.

Short hair is bad. Mark of a prisoner, a cop, or a wage slave.

Smoking is bad.
Marijuana is good.
Sex is good.
Sexual abstinence is insane.

He is now sitting against the wall, talking quietly. The red glow flickers on His round glasses. He is a mad saint.

At the higher levels of energy, beyond even the electronic, there is no form. Form is pure energy limiting itself. Form is error.

On one trip they (I'll refer to "they" for lack of a better term), the higher intelligence, beckoned me to leave the living form and to merge with the eternal formless which is all form, and I was tempted. Eternal ecstasy. But I declined regretfully. I wanted to stay in this form for a while longer.

Why?

Oh, to make love. Balling is such a friendly, tender, human thing to do.

How about eating?

Oh, yes, that's tender, too.

Okay. Let's go to a restaurant.

Owsley is a highly conscious man. He is aware at all times of who he is and what's what. Aware of his mythic role. Aware of his past incarnations. Aware of his animal heritage which he wears, preeningly and naturally, like a pure forest creature. His sense of smell. Owsley carefully selects and blends perfumes for himself and his friends. Your nose always recognizes Owsley. Oh, some sandalwood, a dash of musk, a touch of lotus, a taste of civet.

I talked to Him once on the phone after a session. He was in His customary state of intense excitement. "Listen, man, I saw clearly my mystic Karmic assignment. I am Merlin. I'm a mischievous alchemist. A playful redeemer. My essence name is A.O.S.3."

Like any successful wizard, A.O.S.3 is a good scientist. Radar-sensitive in His observations. Exacting, meticulous, pedantic about His procedures. He has grandiose delusions about the quality of His acid. "Listen, man, LSD is a delicate, fragile molecule. It responds to the vibrations of the chemist."

He judges acid and other psychedelics with the fussy, patron-
izing skill of a Bordeaux wine taster. He is less than kind to
upstart rival alchemists. But no jeweler, goldsmith, painter,
sculptor, was ever more scrupulous about aesthetic perfection
than A.O.S.3.

And like any good journeyman-messiah, His sociological and
political perceptions are arrow straight. As do all turned-on
persons, A.O.S.3 agonizes over the pollution of the living
fabric. He, as well as anyone, sees the mechanization. The
robotization.

Metal is good. It performs its own technical function. Metal
has individuality, soul.

Plastics are evil. Plastic copies the form of plant, mineral,
metal, flesh but has no soul.

Owsley's life is a fierce protest against the sickness of our
times which inverts man and nature into frozen, brittle plastic.
Only a turned-on chemist can appreciate the horror, the ultimate blasphemous horror of plastic.

Owsley is unique. He is himself. His life is a creative struggle
for individuality. He longs for a social group, a linkage of minds
modeled after the harmonious collaboration of cells and organs
of the body. He wants to be the brains of a social love body. The
ancient utopian hunger. Only a turned-on chemist can appreciate God's protein plan for society.

A.O.S.3 is that rare species, a realized, living, breathing,
smelling, balling, laughing, working, scolding man. A ridiculous, conceited fool, God's fool, dreaming of ways to make us all
happy, to turn us all on, to love us and be loved.

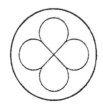

SEAL OF THE LEAGUE

5

M.I.T. Is T.I.M. Spelled Backward*

It was a beautiful autumn Saturday, with the leaves at their psychedelic best, as we drove up to the large mansion which Dr. Leary and his 30 religious cohorts call home. We arrived as a house meeting was breaking up.

Dr. Leary was in his normal dress (white shirt, white slacks and red socks) and was quite warm and receptive. A half-hour delay before the interview gave us time to take in his home and meet some of the workers, who were preparing for the upcoming Tuesday celebration at New York's Village Theater.

The house was beautifully well kept, with a minimum of traditional furniture and a pleasant abundance of creative artwork all around. The faded tapestries of a flower-type design that had covered the walls for decades were attractively renovated with bright paint in many colors. Even the pay phone in the stairwell was painted in weird green swirls. On the wall next to the door on the way out was an appropriate sign saying, "Those who don't know talk, and those who know don't talk."

The house was alive with small children, whose presence added all the more vitality to the place. The older workers, most of them our age, seemed generally affable, good-humored and well-educated, and certainly dedicated to their artistic and religious endeavors.

After a pleasant buffet of apple cider and nonpsychedelic mushrooms over rice with salad, Dr. Leary came down and in-

---

* An interview conducted by Jean Smith and Cynthia White for *Innisfree*, the MIT monthly journal of inquiry, published by Massachusetts Institute of Technology students.

vited us into his office. The half-hour downstairs had broadened our perspectives, but the greatest broadening was yet to come.

INNISFREE: Dr. Leary, one of your comments in your *Playboy* interview was that if you take LSD in a nuthouse, you will have a nuthouse experience. The modern student seems to be in a rat race and may not feel he can spare more than a day, say a Saturday, for a "trip." If a student were to take LSD in this rat race environment, would he have a rat race experience?

LEARY: Well, you're asking for a wild generalization. No one should take LSD unless he's well prepared, unless he knows what he's getting into, unless he's ready to go out of his mind; and his session should be in a place which will facilitate a positive, serene reaction, and with someone whom he trusts emotionally and spiritually.

INNISFREE: When you were experimenting at Harvard, did you find that students were less prepared to go out of their minds?

LEARY: Well, I never gave drugs to any student at Harvard, contrary to rumor. We did give psychedelic drugs to many graduate students, young professors, and researchers at Harvard. These people were very well trained and prepared for the experience. They were doing it for a serious purpose, that is, to learn more about consciousness, the game of mastering this technique for their own personal life and for their professional work.

INNISFREE: Did you ever publish any of your findings from your Harvard stay?

LEARY: Yes, we have published over 35 scholarly and scientific articles. Many of these were based on our Harvard studies: statistical studies, questionnaire studies, descriptions of our rehabilitation work with prisoners, experimental work in producing visionary and mystical experiences, and so forth.

INNISFREE: One of the greatest areas of controversy in regard to LSD is that many people fear, Professor Teuber at MIT for one, that from taking LSD you might have recurrences of the psychosis without further ingestion of the drug. Would you like to comment on this?

LEARY: Number one, I can't agree with the word *psychosis.*

The aim of taking LSD is to develop yourself spiritually and to open up greater sensitivity. Therefore the aim should be to continue after the session the exciting process you have begun. We're delighted when people tell us that after their LSD sessions they can recapture some of the illumination and the meaning and the beauty. Psychiatrists think they are creating psychoses; therefore, they would be alarmed at having the experience persist. We know that we are producing religious experiences, and we and our subjects aim to have those experiences endure. And if Professor Teuber's worried about the fact that nobody knows exactly what LSD does, and I share that worry, we must realize that scientifically we are not sure of what thousands of energies which we ingest or surround ourselves by are doing: gas fumes, DDT, penicillin, tranquilizers. Nobody knows how these work, what effects they'll have not only on the individual but also on the genetic structure of the species. There are risks involved whenever you take LSD. Nobody should take LSD unless he know's he's going into the unknown. He's laying his blue chips on the line. He's tampering with that most delicate and sacred of all instruments, the human brain. You should know that. But you know that you're taking a risk every time you breathe the air, every time you eat the food that the supermarkets are putting out, every time you fall in love for that matter.

Life is a series of risks. We insist only that the person who goes into it knows that it's a risk, knows what's involved, and we insist also that we have the right to take that risk. No paternalistic society and no paternalistic profession like medicine has the right to prevent us from taking that risk. If you listen to neurologists and psychiatrists, you'd never fall in love.

INNISFREE: A friend of ours told us that he had recurring hallucinations at a time when he really didn't want them and didn't expect them. Are these uncontrollable replays common?

LEARY: I think that everyone who takes LSD is permanently changing his consciousness. That is, there are going to be recurrent memories and recurrent reactions when you hear the same music, when you're with the same people, when you walk into the same room. Any stimulation may set off a memory. Now a memory is a live, chemical-molecular event in your nervous system. When you take LSD, you're changing that system to a small degree. Now most people are delighted when this happens.

In any thousand people, or perhaps hundred, there's a professional full-time worrier. Now when this person takes LSD, he's going to wonder if he's going crazy, he's going to worry that he's insane, he's going to worry about brain damage, he's going to worry about controlling it. Worriers, of course, are people who want to have everything under control. And life is not under control. Life is a spontaneous, undisciplined, unsupervised event. Your worrying person is going to lay his worrying machinery on LSD.

INNISFREE: You mentioned religion a few minutes ago. Professor Huston Smith of MIT has suggested that the drug-induced religious experience may not be a truly genuine one.

LEARY: You're now sitting in a religious center. About 30 people are devoting their lives and energies to a full-time pursuit of the Divinity through the sacrament of LSD. You're calling our sacramental experience psychotic. LSD, the psychedelic experience, is a religious experience. It can be if the person is looking for it, and can be if the person is not looking for it and doesn't want it. Professor Smith has on several occasions stated his belief that the drug-induced experience is a religious experience. He has questions, as I understand it, about how this can be used and how well we are applying our religious experiences, but he does not doubt that they are religious experiences. Now the religious experience is beyond any creed or ritual, any myth or metaphor. People use different interpretations, different metaphors to describe their religious experience. A Christian person will take LSD and report it in terms of the Christian vocabulary. Buddhists will do likewise.

INNISFREE: Is it true that you yourself are Hindu?

LEARY: Our religious philosophy, or our philosophy about the spiritual meaning of LSD, comes closer to Hinduism than to any other. Hinduism—again, it is difficult to define Hinduism—recognizes the divinity of all manifestations of life, physical, physiological, chemical, biological, and so forth. So that the Hindu point of view allows for a wide scope of subsects. To a Hindu, Catholicism is a form of Hinduism.

INNISFREE: Your descriptions of the psychedelic experience sound very much like Hermann Hesse's *Siddhartha*. How much have you been influenced by his writings?

LEARY: We've been influenced very much by Hermann Hesse's writings. Of course, once you finally get into the field of consciousness, in the philosophic and literary interpretations of the consciousness, then everyone agrees. Everyone is in basic agreement about the necessity of going out of your mind, going within, and about what you find once you get there. The metaphors change from culture to culture. The terminology is different. But every great mystic and every great missionary reports essentially the same thing: the eternal flow, timeless series of evolutions, and so forth, and Hermann Hesse is one of the great visionary spokesmen of the twentieth century. We made it very explicit in our first psychedelic celebration in New York that we were addressing ourselves to the intellectual who is entrapped in his mind, and we were using as our bible for that first celebration *Steppenwolf,* by Hermann Hesse. The next psychedelic celebration was based on the life of Christ, and we used the Catholic missal as the manual for that. But each one of these great myths is based on a psychedelic experience, a death-rebirth sequence.

INNISFREE: Is each of these sessions supposed to appeal to a different kind of person?

LEARY: Each celebration will take up one of the greatest religious traditions. And we attempt to turn on everyone to that religion. And we hope that anyone that comes to all of our celebrations will discover the deep meaning that exists in each of these. But in addition to that, we hope that the Christian will be particularly turned on by our Catholic LSD mass, because it will renew for him the metaphor which for most of us has become rather routine and tired.

INNISFREE: Where did you get for your foundation the name Castalia?

LEARY: Castalia was taken from Hermann Hesse's novel *Magister Ludi*. The Castalia brotherhood in that novel was one of scientist-scholars who were attempting to bring together visionary mysticism and modern science and scholarship. They would also meditate and use the techniques of the East in order to bring together the bead game itself, a means of weaving together poetry, music, mathematics, science, and unifying them. We attempt to do the same. Our psychedelic celebrations and the lectures that Dr. Metzner and I have been giving in the last two years are very much like the bead game. We attempt to weave together modern techniques like electronics and modern scientific theories, pharmacology and biogenetics, with many different forms of Eastern psychology. It's very clearly a bead game that we are weaving in these celebrations. The aim is to turn on not just the mind, but to turn on the sense organs, and even to talk to people's cells and ancient centers of wisdom.

INNISFREE: Yet, a lot of your beliefs do borrow from other cultures. Wouldn't exposure to these other ways of thinking make your religion more meaningful?

LEARY: Well, I was born in the twentieth century. I can't wipe out my whole personal background or change the fact that almost everyone I talk to today is brain-damaged by our education. We're all crippled. We have to accept the fact that in primary school we fell into the hands of addictive drug pushers, namely teachers. They've crippled us. That's part of karma.

Every historical era has its own particular trap which drives man away from his divinity and puts him on the outside, and every historical era has its own sacrament, or its own method, of dealing with it. The DNA code is an impressively resilient and impressive blueprinting process. It always produces the protein molecules that are necessary to adapt to the particular evolutionary bind it has actually trapped itself in. Evolution is a series of accidental surprises.

The genetic code is infinite in its variation and wisdom, and always comes out with the right answer; and exactly the right answer for the particular neurological disease that man has been plagued by for the last 1,000 years is LSD. You see, 3,000 or

4,000 years ago, LSD wouldn't have been necessary. Man was in touch. He was harmoniously dancing along with the change in the planets, the change in the seasons. He was in touch, he was in tune, he was turned on. LSD existed in natural form. LSD has been in morning glory seeds for hundreds of thousands of years. But until now it hasn't been necessary to use because you wouldn't have had to have the effect.

INNISFREE: You don't feel that the LSD culture is compatible with American culture now, then?

LEARY: I don't think the American culture is compatible with anything. Certainly not with anything that's been going on in this planet since the origin of life. The American culture is an insane asylum. You take for granted such things as race prejudice, the Protestant work culture, the professional bureaucracy which exists in this country, the complete loss of euphoria which has developed in the past fifty years. Dropping bombs on natives of Vietnam—well, that's just like a head cold. I mean, that's the way it's supposed to be. It's the current symptom of our insanity.

LSD and the LSD cult is perfectly in tune with the wisdom of the Buddha or the great philosophies of the past. The Buddha could walk up this road to our house here at Millbrook, and he'd see the signs of his profession because we belong to the same profession, people who are changing consciousness, who are pursuing the eternal quest. He would walk in this house and he'd be much more at home here than he would be in hardly any house in the United States because we're in touch with him. We're in touch with the basic cellular and sensory and physical aspects of man.

There are three processes involved that every spiritual teacher has passed onto mankind for the past thousand years. Look within, have the revelation, and then express it in acts of glorification on the outside and detach yourself from the current tribe. We use the six-word motto "Turn on, tune in, drop out." Now after you turn on, you don't spend the rest of your life in an LSD state, just contemplating the inner wonders. You begin immediately expressing your revelation in acts of beauty without. That's what we're doing in the Village Theater in New York. Every Tuesday night, people come there and we stone them out of their minds.

INNISFREE: What about LSD?

LEARY: Well, it's always biochemical. In order to do anything new, you have to change your nervous system biochemically. Now you can do it through breathing, fasting, flagellation, dancing, solitude, diet. You can do it through any sense organ— visual, auditory, and so forth. There are hundreds of ways of turning on. But at the present time, man is so sick that there are very few people who can use these ancient methods, so that today it is safe to say that drugs are the specific, and almost the only, way that the American is ever going to have a religious experience.

And our Tuesday night celebrations do not take the place of the sacrament. The sacramental process in our religion is the use of marijuana and LSD; and nothing can substitute for that. There's a way of training people, and a way of teaching people, and a way of demonstrating to people what the psychedelic does. We have these public celebrations.

INNISFREE: You don't seem, then, to be advocating the use of LSD for simple "kicks."

LEARY: I don't know what you mean by "kicks." We feel about LSD the way a Catholic priest feels about his host. He doesn't want to have his host sold in vending machines. He doesn't want to have his sacred host in the hands of doctors to decide who's going to use it. He wants his host to be given by trained priests or guides in the temple. We feel exactly the same about LSD. Now, the Catholic host should indeed give you a kick. LSD will give you a kick. The kick to me means an ecstatic revelation. I don't know what a kick means to you. To you a kick may mean going to a cocktail party in Cambridge and flirting with some girl. A kick to me means flirtation—confrontation—with God. Of course, in our puritan society, the word *kick* is a negative term. We're such robots that we think the only thing we should do in life is work, get power, and use this power to control other people. In any sane society, the word *kick* could be the ideal. Kick is the ecstacy; it means going beyond, confronting God, getting out of your mind.

INNISFREE: What would LSD achieve, though, that conscientious Hindu-like meditation—if we were capable of it—could not achieve?

LEARY: If meditation works, it will get you the same place that LSD will. But only one person in a hundred thousand can do it through meditation.

INNISFREE: Even to what you call the precellular level of awareness?

LEARY: Well, certainly the Buddha, and certainly the writings of the Hindu philosophers—the Shiva myths—were written by men who had reached the cellular level. The theory of reincarnation in Hinduism is a perfect metaphorical and poetic statement of the DNA code.

INNISFREE: What of the actual biochemical changes that are behind the psychedelic experience?

LEARY: Neurologists do not understand the biochemistry of consciousness. They don't know where consciousness is located. Therefore, the answer to the question of, "What does LSD do?" has to await a breakthrough in neurology. And that breakthrough in neurology will come when neurologists realize that they have to change their *own* consciousness. They're not going to find out where consciousness is located by putting electrodes in the brains of animals or giving LSD to animals for that matter. The breakthrough in neurology is going to come when the scientist puts his eye to the microscope; and the microscope of consciousness is your own nervous system. We have trained hundreds of young graduate students, who are now young psychiatrists and young neurologists, and this next generation of turned-on scientists will produce the great breakthrough in neurology, because they are taking the drug themselves.

INNISFREE: Do you think that the two sciences can coexist side by side?

LEARY: There's a perfect dialogue that goes on between outer and inner. It doesn't do any good to expand your consciousness unless you can accurately express this in some metaphorical or symbolic form. Now the problem at the present time is that our society and our intellectuals and our scientists completely externalize the psychology of behaviorism. Neurology today is poking at the brains of other people. We're overbalanced this way today. As soon as psychiatrists start taking LSD or more powerful drugs that come along, they will be tuning in on an energy process that will then help them write better equations. You have to experience what you are symbolizing. And when a symbol system gets beyond the experience, then it becomes just a chess game.

When Einstein first worked out that equation $E=MC^2$, it was a very powerful, psychedelic thing. Literally he had to fall down on his knees at that moment when he realized that all matter was energy just in temporary states of change, that there was no structure. Of course, the Hindu philosophers had pointed that out for a thousand years. But I suspect that very few physicists experience what they are symbolizing.

You see, that's the problem. I think that 99 percent of the people who call themselves scientists, including 99 percent of the people at your institution, are not really scientists. There are never more than a hundred people who deserve the term *scientist* in any age. The rest of them are just engineers who are simply playing out one little aspect of a metaphor, of a visionary experience, that someone had in the past.

INNISFREE: How do you determine whether a person will become psychotic under LSD? Is there any way to tell who had best not participate in this religion? Because surely not everyone can.

LEARY: Who's to decide? I would say that at present our society is so insane, that even if the risks were fifty-fifty that if you took LSD you would be permanently insane, I still think that the risk is worth taking, as long as the person knows that that's the risk.

There is a complete breakdown in assumption here. You're operating from a psychiatric metaphor, and I'm operating from a religious metaphor. I say that the confrontation with divinity is going to change you, and there are some people who are in such a state of sin that they don't want to confront divinity; they freak out. Such people should be warned that if you come into this temple you're going to face blazing illumination of the divinity. It's going to change you completely; you're never going to be the same. Do you want to do it? That's what they said in the Eleusinian Mysteries. They would always warn people, "If you go in here, you will die. You and all of your past hang-ups, sins and so forth are going to be laid out in front of you. You're going to have to confront them, strip them off and be a changed person. Do you want to do it?" One of the emperors of Rome—I forget which one—came and wanted to be initiated in the Eleusinian Mysteries, and they took him in and said, "This is what's going to happen," and he said, "That's interesting. I approve of what you're doing, but I don't want your experience. I don't want to be changed." As long as the person knows what's involved, whatever he does to his own consciousness is his own business. And the fears of LSD in this society existed before the present psychiatric rumors of brain damage. Everyone is afraid to take LSD, because nobody wants to change. Everyone wants to keep his own little egocentric chess game going. The fear of LSD is the same fear that has led to the persecution of people doing the same thing I've been doing in other centuries and other tribes. It's the ancient game of the law. Three hundred years ago you'd be sitting here talking with me about the devil. In Salem, very close to where you go to college, they were talking about witches. The fear then was in terms of witches. The fear of those who are anti-God—which is what you are—the fear is always expressed in the metaphor of the time: witches, possessions, devils, and so forth.

INNISFREE: You have no fear of LSD?

LEARY: I didn't say that, nor would I. There's everything to fear. You're going to lose your mind.

INNISFREE: Isn't there the fear of taking too much?

LEARY: There is no lethal dose known of LSD. LSD is a trigger mechanism, like a key. So, ten times the normal dose of LSD is like ten keys for one lock. When you get over three hundred gammas of LSD, you can go up to thirty thousand gammas—the largest dose I know of—and the impact is a little greater: the door swings open a little faster. But it's the same effect. You see, what you're confronting is your own two-billion-year-old equipment of sense organs, cellular wisdom, protein memories. They're the same. Our culture is so hung on the external, playing the numbers game, that 1,000 gammas must be twice as strong as 500 gammas.

INNISFREE: If you cannot get back to the state where you can contemplate on what you have just experienced, wouldn't you consider that bad?

LEARY: The problem with LSD is not enduring change. The problem is that it doesn't last long enough. You see, if LSD really worked the way these fear merchants say it does, it would be easy to use it to change personality. If it changes the normal person and gives him hallucinations afterward, you should be able to take the criminal and the alcoholic, the drug addict, and the generally mean person and change him under guidance. The processes of neurological imprinting and the way we build up our conditioned mental processes is highly resistant to change. If you take LSD, you still come back speaking the English language and knowing how to tie your shoe lace. The problem with LSD is that much too quickly do you slip back into the routine ways of thinking. That's why, if you take LSD, you should take it many, many times, and you should plan to slowly change your environment so that your external commitments are keeping up to your internal achievements. It's very hard work to change the human psychology, even with LSD. That should give comfort to the frightened, and probably anguish to the optimistic like myself. Human nature is so resistant to change.

INNISFREE: Do you think you are being harassed for your unorthodox beliefs?

LEARY: I don't use the term *harassment,* and I have no paranoid theories about conspiracy. The game I am involved in is set out with exquisite precision. What I am doing has been done by people in every generation in the past. It's like the Harvard-Yale game. It's played out every year. Now, Harvard isn't harassing Yale. The game between those who know that man can change and become divine in this lifetime and want tó teach people how to do it completely threatens the establishment. In every generation you say, "No, it's all been done and settled, and just get your good lawyer-priest and do what we tell you to do." And this dialogue between the establishment and the utopian visionaries will inevitably exist in every historical era.

It's played fairly. The fact that they want to hound me out of existence is right. They should, just like the Harvard defensive team wants to throw the offensive's quarterback for a loss. I have no complaint about this; I'm perfectly good-humored about it. The more energy that is directed against me, the more energy that is available for me. It's the perfect physical law of jujitsu—the more government and professional establishment dynamism that is set off against what we're doing is just a sign to us that we're doing fine.

INNISFREE: What are the existing restrictions on LSD by the federal government?

LEARY: The federal law does not forbid the possession and personal use of LSD. It prohibits the manufacture and sale of LSD or the administering of it to someone. There are some states—four or five, of which New York State is one—which outlaw the possession of LSD.

INNISFREE: In your *Playboy* interview you gave the exact number of LSD sessions you had taken. You record each session?

LEARY: Yes, I keep careful record of each session, where, and what was the purpose of the session.

INNISFREE: And do you write down a description of the experience or thoughts that came to you?

LEARY: Yes, most of the time. Not always.

INNISFREE: What do you consider more valuable, the actual trip or the contemplation of it afterward?

LEARY: It goes together. One without the other is rather meaningless. But again, you ask if I write it down. It's more important what you *do* afterward; after a session we may go out and plant a new garden, after a session we may change a room in the house, after a session we may throw out the television set, after the session I may spend the next five hours talking quietly with my son. The intellectual is so hung up on the disease of words that nothing exists unless he writes it down. The human being has been involved in this adventure for thousands of years before the printing press. As my friend Marshall McLuhan so eloquently pointed out—you see, whatever I say today about words is just what Marshall McLuhan said in his book, *The Gutenberg Galaxie*—the misuse of the printing press is one of the greatest catastrophes to happen to the human nervous system. It has forced man to think in the linear subject-predicate fashion, which is what Marshall McLuhan and I are attempting to do something about, and which modern technical advances, like electronics, and psychochemicals such as LSD, will inevitably change.

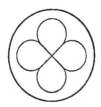

SEAL OF THE LEAGUE

6

*The Buddha as Drop-Out**

The message of the Buddha, Gautama, is the familiar, ancient always to-be-rediscovered divine instruction:

Drop out

Turn on

Tune in

The avatar, the divine one, is he who discovers and lives out this rhythm during his earthly trip.

The life of the Buddha, Gautama, is simply another case illustration in the venerable library of tissue manuals on "How to Discover Your Own Buddha-hood."

Gautama Sakyamuni was born a prince. His father, the king, and his mother, the queen, were determined that he should carry on the family business and not discover his divinity. According to familiar parental tradition, they attempted to protect their son from confronting the four basic dimensions of the human time span: sickness, age, death, and the existence of

---

* This article was written in response to a request from *Horizon* magazine, which in the summer of 1967 was planning an issue on the hippies.

The article was penciled hastily and typed by the author's daughter, who at the time was involved in a mystical removal from all human games except the mastery of touch typing.

Horizon sent a check for $400 along, with a note of puzzling jocularity about my "frankness" and "honesty." It was only after the issue was published (without "The Buddha as Drop-Out") and after reading the introduction to the issue that it became clear that the editors of lost *Horizon* had mirthlessly missed the point of the article. They saw it as confessional rather than satirical. They wanted no part in the strategy to persuade their readers to become Buddhas.

They have a point. Buddhas don't subscribe. They inscribe.

eccentric, barefoot holy men—alchemists who could show him
how to solve the time riddle by—

Dropping out

Turning on

Tuning in

The truth of the matter is that the Buddha was born and
brought up in Westchester County, educated at an Ivy League
college and groomed for that pinnacle of princely success which
would allow him in 1967 to subscribe to *Horizon,* a magazine
particularly unlikely to confront him with the prospect of his
own divinity.

First Gautama dropped out. Horrors! Did he really desert his
wife and child? Run out on the palace mortgage payment?
Welsh on his commitments to his 10,000 concubines? Leave the
Internal Revenue Service holding the bag for the Vietnam War
bill? Maybe he just moved with his wife and kids to Big Sur, not
even leaving a forwarding address for fourth-class mail. Lost
Horizon. Or maybe the drop-out was internal (where it always
has to be). Maybe he just detached himself invisibly from the
old fears and ambitions.

After his drop-out he struggled to turn on. It's never easy,
you know, to turn on. He memorized the Vedas. Read the
Upanishads and the *Village Voice* and Alan Watts and Krish-
namurti. Studied at the feet of gurus. Got the message. "Sorry,
young man. We can't teach it. Divinity is a do-it-yourself propo-
sition, located somewhere inside your own body."

So he spent several years practicing lonely austerities. Diet
and physical yoga. Gave up smoking. Ate macrobiotic rice. Got
thin. Let his beard grow. Looked holy but felt wholly terrible.

One day, as he was sitting under a tree, a dairy maid offered
him a bowl of milk and honey, maybe laced with mushroom
juice. It was a forbidden, dangerous potion, against all the laws
of yoga abstinence.

Then he started his trip. Session delights. The marijuana
miracle! Vision! Touch! Smell! Sound! Beautiful! Ecstasy!!!
But don't get caught, Buddha! All the manuals warn you!
Center your mind! Float to the beginning!

Next came the sexual visions. Mara the devil sent his naked daughters to entrance. The devil, you say? Oh, didn't they tell you in Bronxville Sunday School and the comparative religions seminar at Princeton that the devil is part of your own mind that wants you to cop out and sell short your timeless divinity? You're a junior executive now with the narcotic security needle hooked in your liberal Republican vein, and the secretaries at the office think you're cute Mr. Horizon-reading Buddha. But remember the teachings! Enjoy but don't chase the erotic fantasies. Center!

Then came the terrors. You'll go insane! You'll lose your ambition! Brain damage! Permanent psychosis! Bellevue Hospital! Chromosome destruction! Jump out a palace window! Who are you, anyway? Spoiled prince, arrogant Brooks Brothers Faust, to grab with greedy hands the delicate web of God? You're crazy now and will never get back. Help! Paranoia! Call the court physician! Call a psychiatrist!

But Gautama remembered the prayer. He centered his mind and body. He spun through the thousand past reincarnations. Tumbled down his DNA code and died, merging in the center of the solar, lunar, diamond, peacock eye of fire that men call God. Illumination.

From whence he looked back up and saw the fibrous unfolding of life to come, all past, all future, hooked up, the riddle of time and mortality solved by the unitive, turn-on perspective.

And at that moment of highest Samhadi, Gautama opened his eyes in delight and wonder at the paradise rediscovered by his trip, and looked around and said that great line—"Wonder of all wonders, all men are the Buddha."

He had dropped out and turned on. He had made it to the navel-centered beginning. Realized the Buddha-nature of all creatures. And then what? The crossroads in the heroic-mythic-God trip. Why come down? Once you've seen it all, experienced the divine flash, why return to the frayed uniform and clumsy tools of your earthly games? How can you come down to play out a role in the silly TV drama of American society? How can you come down from the Buddha game? The wholly-man role?

I read the blues today, oh, boy, about a lucky man who great the made.*

Tradition has it that Gautama Buddha after his illumination sat for days under the bo tree, wondering whether he should come back to deal with the pompous Brahmin priesthood and his kindly but myopic parents, the aging king and queen, and the FDA at Benares and the crowd back at the office and the shallow hit-and-run celestial aspirations of his followers. Or even to write articles for the well-meaning editors of very slick magazines. Why bother?

Gautama's question is exactly that anguishing dilemma faced by several million young Americans who have taken the psychedelic trip in the last 5 years. Because, when seen *sub specie aeternitatis*, American society really does appear quite destructive and insane. What can LBJ or Billy Graham offer a dropped-out, turned-on, ill-prepared, confused teen-ager visionary?

Why not stay dropped out?

Perhaps the wisest of our times are the total drop-outs—those eccentrics who look around and fold their hands and quit. The quietly but shrewdly mad who crowd our mental hospitals. The drifting, smiling, welfare checksters.

But the message of the Buddha is to tune in. Glorify! Tune back in, not to the old game. You have to stay dropped out of that. You drop back in to life. You come back down and express your revelation in acts of glory and beauty and humor. Help someone else drop out and turn on.

The Buddha dropped back in with his four noble truths:

All life is suffering.

The suffering is caused by striving.

You can end the suffering by dropping out of the chase.

The dropping out involves an eightfold discipline, hard work, continual attention, constant centering of consciousness.

The term "drop-out" is, of course, deliberately distorted by Brahmins, bureaucrats, moralists, politicians and external power holders. They know that their control will fall apart if people drop out and turn on. The brahminical federal strategy

* Paraphrased from a classic Buddhist text published by the Beatles.

has always been the same. Convince the people that the TV show emanating from Benares, Athens, Rome, London, Saigon, Washington is reality and that the ecstasy is an escape into psychosis and irresponsibility.

The fact of the matter, as Gautama's career makes very clear, is that dropping out is the demanding, arduous road. The lonely, scary confrontation with the evolutionary reality. The narcotic escape is to remain in the system. Be a good king, young Buddha. Raise taxes. Encourage trade. Fight wars to protect your people against the enemy. Be good. Join the Christian meddling, missionary society of your time. Of necessity, be a good rebel and protest, picket, lobby, for the political power of the "outs." The oldest cop-out of history. Nice rebel!

The message of the Gautama Sakyamuni is drop out and turn on. You can't *do* good until you *feel* good. You can't free others until *you* are free.

Gautama, the Nepalese drop-out, is the greatest spiritual master of recorded history. His message is bleak and direct. Each man is Buddha. The aim of human life is to discover your Buddha-hood. You must do this yourself. You can't rely on any of the divine avatars of the past. Jesus is dead. Krishna is dead. Lao-tse is gone. You must retrace the ancient path yourself. Discover your own Christ-hood. Stagger down from the mountain, flipped-out Moses, with your own moral code fashioned in the ecstatic despair of your own revelation. The only help you have is the teaching. Fashion a prayer and keep your sense of humor. Use the guidebooks and manuals left by the inspired drop-outs of the past. The Buddha himself spent forty years teaching the most accurate and detailed psychological system the world has ever known. This was his tuning-back-in exercise. Use it and go beyond it.

But the old texts mainly tell you what not to do. The timing, the direction, the style, the rhythm, the ritual of your search is for you to evolve. But this much is known. It's all right. It's all worked out. It's all on autopilot. Remember the Buddha message. Turn on, tune in, drop out.

Remember the Buddha smile.

Dear *Horizon* reader, put your finger on this
   dot

●

'

remember, and smile.

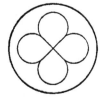

SEAL OF THE LEAGUE

7

Homage to Huxley

November 22, 1963, was for Aldous Huxley the time to go.

In paying tribute (a curious word) to a departed luminary, it is customary to appraise his contribution, to wrap up the meaning and message of the hero and to place it with a flourish in the inactive file.

This ceremonial function is notoriously risky in the case of writers. The literary game has its own stock-exchange quotations in which hardcover commodities rise and fall to the irrational dictates of scholarly fashion.

To predict the place that Aldous Huxley will have as a literary figure is a gambling venture we shall leave to the professionals who are paid to do it. They might note that he did not win a Nobel Prize—a good sign, suggesting that he made the right enemies and was properly unacceptable to the academic politicians. They will note also that he was a visionary—always a troublesome issue to the predictor. Since all visionaries say the same thing, they are perennial commodities, difficult to sell short, annoyingly capable of turning up fresh and alive a thousand years later.

But Aldous Huxley is not just a literary figure, and for that matter not just a visionary writer. Which adds to the critic's problem. The man just wouldn't stop and pose for the definitive portrait. He just wouldn't slide symmetrically into an academic pigeonhole. What shall we call him? Sage? Wise teacher? Calypso guru? Under what index heading do we file the smiling prophet? The nuclear age bodhisattva?

Many of the generation of scholars and critics who presently adjudicate literary reputations received their first insights into the snobbish delights of the mind from the early novels of Huxley.

> I believe that no one under fifty can quite realize how exciting Huxley seemed to us who were schoolboys or undergraduates in the 'twenties . . . he was a popularizer of what, at the time, were "advanced" ideas . . . he was a liberator, who seemed to encourage us in our adolescent revolt against the standards of our parents.[1]

This obituary appraisal, a nice example of the "cracked looking glass" school of literary criticism, continues in the same vein:

> I remained under the Huxleyan enchantment well into my twenties. The magic began gradually to fail after *Point Counter Point* (1928) ; its failure was due partly to my discovery of other contemporary writers (Proust, Joyce, Lawrence) , partly to the fact that Huxley himself had by that time lost something of his original sparkle. I felt little sympathy for his successive preoccupations with scientific utopias, pacifism, and Yoga. . . .

Of all the misunderstandings which divide mankind, the most tragic, obvious, and vicious is the conflict between the young and the old. It is surely not Huxley who lost his sparkle but perhaps the quoted critic, who graduated from "adolescent revolt" (a dubious, ungracious, middle-aged phrase) to a static "postadolescent" fatigue with new ideas. Huxley continued to produce prose which sparkled, to those who could transfer their vision from the mirror to the events which were occurring around them.

I believe that no one over fifty can quite realize how exciting

1 Jocelyn Brooke, "The Wicked Uncle: An Appreciation of Aldous Huxley," *The Listener,* Vol. LXX, No. 1811 (December 12, 1963) , p. 991.

Huxley seems to the generations which followed their own. The early Huxley was the urbane sophisticate who taught naïve youngsters that parental notions about sex and society left something to be improved. The early Huxley was an exciting coach in the game of intellectual one-upmanship, wickedly demonstrating how to sharpen the mind so that it could slice experience into categories, how to engage in brilliant, witty repartee, how to be a truly sophisticated person.

But "then came *Brave New World* (1932), an entirely new departure, and not, I think, a happy one. . . ." Yes, indeed. Then comes the grim new world of the 1930's and a new generation who were less concerned with sparkling conversation than with trying to figure out why society was falling apart at the seams. The game of polishing your own mind and developing your own personality (although kept alive in the rituals of psychoanalysis) starts to look like narcissistic chess. Huxley was one of the first men of his times to see the limitations of the obsession with self and never again wrote to delight the intellectual.

But old uncles are supposed to keep their proper place in *my* picture album. They have no right charging off in new directions. Investigating meta-self social ideas and meta-self modes of consciousness. No right to calmly ask the terrible new questions of the mind: Is this all? Shakespeare and Joyce and Beethoven and Freud—is there no more? Television and computers—is this all? Uncle Aldous, who taught us how to be clever, rational, individualistic, now claims that our sharp minds are creating air-conditioned, test-tube anthills. "As Mr. Cyril Connolly put it, 'Science had walked off with art,' and a latent streak of vulgarity found expression. . . ." Yes, the specific prophecy *is* vulgar.

And what is even more tasteless—to be so right. Within 15 years the ludicrous, bizarre mechanization of new world fantasy had become a reality. The conventional artistic response to automation is the nihilist protest. But again Aldous Huxley refuses to play the literary game, insists on tinkering with evolutionary resolutions. Some of us forgot that Uncle Aldous was also grandson. The extra-ordinary, dazzling erudition which spun out *bons mots* in the early novels is now sifting through the wisdom of the East.

Huxley's diplomatic journey to the East brings back no final answer but the right questions. He seeks the liberating seed while avoiding the deciduous underbrush of ritual.

The first question: Is there more? Need the cortex be limited to the tribal-verbal? Must we use only a fraction of our neurological heritage? Must our minds remain flimsy toys compared to the wisdom within the neural network? How to expand consciousness beyond the learned mind? How to find and teach the liberation from the cultural self? Where are the educational techniques for exploiting the potentials? Here again Huxley avoids doctrinaire digressions into mood, authority, semantics, ritual. He keeps moving, looking for the key which works.

In 1954 he announces the discovery of the Eastern passage: *Doors to Perception, Heaven and Hell.* Psychedelic drugs can provide the illumination, the key to the mind's antipodes, the transcendental experience. You may not want to make the voyage. You may have no interest in transcending your cultural mind. Fine. Don't take LSD. Or you may want illumination but object to the direct, shortcut approach. You prefer the sweat-tears of verbal exercises and rituals. Fine. Don't take LSD. But for those who can accept the "gratuitous grace," there it is.

The age-long problem of how to "get out" has finally been solved. Biochemical mysticism is a demonstrated fact. Next comes the second problem. There is the infused vision of the open cortex, flashing at speeds which far outstrip our verbal machinery. And there is the tribal marketplace which cannot utilize or even allow the accelerated neural energy. How can the gap be bridged?

Aldous Huxley preached no escape from the insanity and semantic madness of the twentieth century. His next message was not one of quietism and *arhat* passivity. No one was more concerned, more engaged, more involved in the active attempt to make the best of both worlds.

To make the best of both worlds—this was the phrase we heard him repeat over and over again during the last years. Of course most of his readers and critics didn't know what he was talking about. If you don't realize that it is now a simple matter to reach ecstasy, to get out, to have the vision, to reach the other worlds of your own cortex, then technical discussions of "re-entry" problems make little sense to you.

But there it was. The old Mahayana question now made real and practical. How to apply the now available potentialities of the accelerated cortex?

Aldous Huxley's last message to the planet contains the answer to this question in the form of the utopian novel *Island*.[2]

This book, published in 1962, is the climax of the 69-year voyage of discovery. It is a great book. It will become a greater book.

Like all great books it is misunderstood in its time because it is so far in front of its time. It's too much to take. Too much. *Island* is a continent, a hemisphere, a galaxy of a book.

At the most superficial level it's a science fiction tale with heroes and villains in a fantasy land. It's a satire as well—of Western civilization and its follies. So far, the book can be dealt with.

But it's much more. It's a utopian tract. Huxley's final statement about how to make the best of both worlds. Of individual freedom and social responsibility. Of East and West. Of left and right cerebral hemispheres. Of action and quietism. Of Tantra and Arhat. Of verbal and nonverbal. Of work and play. Of mind and metamind. Of technique and nature. Of body and spirit. Of religion and the secular.

It's a manual on education. A handbook on psychotherapy and mind control. A solution to the horrors of the biparent family, the monstrous father-mother pressure cooker.

Too much, indeed, for one book; but there's more.

Island is a treatise on living, on the living of each moment.

And most important and staggering, the book is a treatise on dying.

The easy intellectual rejection of this wealth of practical, how-to-do-it information is to call it fantasy. Adolescent daydreams

[2] New York, Harper & Row, 1962.

about how things could be in a society imagined and run by gentle, secluded scholars.

But here is the terrible beauty of Huxley's science-fiction-satirical-utopian manual on how to live and how to live with others and how to die and how to die with others: it's all based on facts. *Island* is a popular presentation of empirical facts—anthropological, psychological, psychedelic, sociological. Every method, every social sequence described in *Island* is based on data. Huxley's utopian ideas can work because they have worked. It's all been done—not in a fantasied future but yesterday.

It has been tried and done by Huxley himself, and by his "Palanese" wife Laura Archera Huxley, who presented many of these intensely practical, down-to-earth ideas in her book, *You Are Not the Target*.[3] It's a mistake to think of him as a detached novelist observing and commenting on the scene. Huxley was a tall, slightly stooped calypso singer, intensely topical, strolling nearsightedly through the crowds, singing funny stilted verses in an English accent, singing about the events in which he was participating. He didn't just figure it out—he experienced much of it himself.

Huxley's explorations with psychedelic drugs are an example of his engagement. His willingness to get involved. Remember, every person who can read without moving his lips has heard about what the *Saturday Evening Post*[4] calls "the dangerous magic of LSD." And despite the controversy, almost everyone knows what is involved—the mind loss and the vision. Everyone has had to come to terms with the new development in his own fashion.

There are as many rational reasons for not taking LSD as there are facets to the human mind—moral, practical, medical, psychiatric, mental. The real reason—however it is expressed—is fear. Fear of losing what we have. Fear of going beyond where we are.

Aldous Huxley had spent years preparing himself for the

[3] New York, Farrar, Straus, 1963.
[4] November 2, 1963.

fearful psychedelic voyage, and he made it without question
when it presented itself. Why? Duty? Curiosity? Conviction?
Courage? Faith in the process? Trust in his companions—divine
or human?

He did it, and the world will never forget it.

But the gamble of the mind was not the last act of faith and
courage. Aldous Huxley went on to face death as he had faced
the whirling enigma of the life process. He tells us about it with
poetic sensitivity and concrete specificity in the fourteenth
chapter of *Island*,* his book of the living and the dying.

Rounding a screen, he [Dr. Robert] caught a glimpse . . .
of a high bed, of a dark emaciated face on the pillow, of arms
that were no more than parchment-covered bones, of claw-like
hands. . . . He looked at the face on the pillow . . . still, still
with a serenity that might almost have been the frozen calm of
death. . . .

"Lakshmi." Susila laid a hand on the old woman's wasted
arm. "Lakshmi," she said again more loudly. The death-calm
face remained impassive. "You mustn't go to sleep."

. . . "Lakshmi!"

The face came to life.

"I wasn't really asleep," the old woman whispered. "It's just
my being so weak. I seem to float away."

"But you've got to be here," said Susila. "You've got to know
you're here. All the time." She slipped an additional pillow
under the sick woman's shoulders and reached for a bottle of
smelling salts that stood on the bed table. . . . Then after
another pause, "Oh, how wonderful," she whispered at last,
"how wonderful!" Suddenly she winced and bit her lip.

Susila took the old woman's hand in both of hers. "Is the
pain bad?" she asked.

"It would be bad," Lakshmi explained, "if it were really my
pain. But somehow it isn't. The pain's here; but I'm somewhere else. It's like what you discover with the *moksha*-
medicine. Nothing really belongs to you. Not even your pain."

. . . "And now," Susila was saying, "think of that view from
the Shiva temple. Think of those lights and shadows on the sea,

* Harper & Row, New York, 1962.

those blue spaces between the clouds. Think of them, and then let go of your thinking. Let go of it, so that the not-Thought can come through. Things into Emptiness, Emptiness into Suchness. Suchness into things again, into your own mind. Remember what it says in the Sutra. 'Your own consciousness shining, void, inseparable from the great Body of Radiance, is subject neither to birth or death, but is the same as the immutable Light, Buddha Amitabha.' "

"The same as the light," Lakshmi repeated. "And yet it's all dark again."

"It's dark because you're trying too hard," said Susila. "Dark because you want it to be light. Remember what you used to tell me when I was a little girl. 'Lightly, child, lightly. You've got to learn to do everything lightly. Think lightly, act lightly, feel lightly. Yes, feel lightly, even though you're feeling deeply.' . . . Lightly, lightly—it was the best advice ever given me. Well, now I'm going to say the same thing to you, Lakshmi . . . Lightly, my darling, lightly. Even when it comes to dying. Nothing ponderous, or portentous, or emphatic. No rhetoric, no tremolos, no self-conscious persona putting on its celebrated imitation of Christ or Goethe or Little Nell. And, of course, no theology, no metaphysics. Just the fact of dying and the fact of the Clear Light. So throw away all your baggage and go forward. There are quicksands all about you, sucking at your feet, trying to suck you down into fear and self-pity and despair. That's why you must walk so lightly. Lightly, my darling . . . Completely unencumbered."

. . . He looked again at the fleshless face on the pillow and saw that it was smiling.

"The Light," came the hoarse whisper, "the Clear Light. It's here—along with the pain, in spite of the pain."

"And where are *you?*" Susila asked.

"Over there, in the corner." Lakshmi tried to point, but the raised hand faltered and fell back, inert, on the coverlet. "I can see myself there. And she can see my body on the bed."

"Can she see the Light?"

"No. The Light's here, where my body is. . . ."

"She's drifted away again," said Susila. "Try to bring her back."

Dr. Robert slipped an arm under the emaciated body and

lifted it into a sitting posture. The head drooped sideways onto his shoulder.

"My little love," he kept whispering. "My little love . . ."

Her eyelids fluttered open for a moment. "Brighter," came the barely audible whisper, "brighter." And a smile of happiness intense almost to the point of elation transfigured her face.

Through his tears Dr. Robert smiled back at her. "So now you can let go, my darling." He stroked her gray hair. "Now you can let go. Let go," he insisted. "Let go of this poor old body. You don't need it any more. Let it fall away from you. Leave it lying here like a pile of worn-out clothes."

In the fleshless face the mouth had fallen cavernously open, and suddenly the breathing became stertorous.

"My love, my little love . . ." Dr. Robert held her more closely. "Let go now, let go. Leave it here, your old worn-out body, and go on. Go on, my darling, go on into the Light, into the peace, into the living peace of the Clear Light . . ."

Susila picked up one of the limp hands and kissed it, then turned. . . .

"Time to go," she whispered. . . .

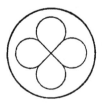

SEAL OF THE LEAGUE

8

The Mad Virgin of Psychedelia

The psychedelic revolution has (with miraculous swiftness) won the hearts and copped the minds of the American people because (like any religious up-heave-all) it uses the ultimate weepon, humor.

Psychedelic guerrillas, disorganized bands of wise goof-offs, creative fuck-ups, and comedian chaplains have in 6 quip years effortlessly taken over the most powerful empire in world history.

With music, clowning, laughter, the psychedelic revolution has passed through the classic sociopolitical stages of every great human renaissance:

1. The philosophic preparation (Alan Watts writes the Zen introduction)

2. The underground swell of the masses hungry for freedom (Allen Ginsberg howls)

3. Accidental flareups of trigger incidents (Laredo, Texas: by this rude bridge that arched the flood, their flag to custom's seize unfurled, here the embattled . . .)

4. Widespread guerrilla tactics (Ken Kesey's Merry Pranksters)

5. The turning-point victory (the publishers of *Time-Life* get turned on)

6. The mopping-up operations (in charge of Sergeant Pepper)

7. The writing of war memoirs, prayer books, manuals, cate-

chisms, new testaments, grandiose biblical versions in which the accidental-inevitable is made to seem planned blueprint

The evangelists and social historians of the psychedelic revolution have a delightful roster of hero-comedian-clowns available for legendary canonization.

Alan Watts is the smiling scholar of the acid age. For 30 years he has been converting the most complex theories of oriental philosophies into jewellike up-levels, wry epigrams. Cool, gracious, never ruffled, chuckling to share with us his amused wonder at God's plans for the planet and, with quizzical eye, glancing to see if we will catch on.

Allen Ginsberg. The celestial clown. Giggling, posturing with complete insight, histrionic, shamelessly direct. No one, not even J. Edgar Hoover, can be with this nearsighted, rumpled, worried, hysterical, lyrical, furry bear for 10 minutes and not giggle back because he tickles and hugs you when no one else dares.

The Leary-Alpert-Metzner-Harvard-Hitchcock-Mellon-Mexico-Millbrook Circus backed and lurched into history, continuously making every mistake except taking itself too seriously for very long. (Someone was always high enough to laugh.) The name of our prisoner-rehabilitation project was "Break-Out." The Good Friday religious experiment became the Miracle of March Chapel—to the dismay of Boston University. And it worked. The initials of our research organization, the International Federation for Internal Freedom, spelled out the conditional paradox of the atomic age. Institutional titles, creeds, were invented and outgrown monthly. Conversion, excommunications, schisms, could never keep up with the changes at Millbrook. You couldn't resign from the Castalia Foundation and denounce its methods because it had already evolved into the League for Social Disorder, which in turn couldn't be sued for its theatrical proceeds because the money and the slide projectors had been given away and everyone was dropped out, camping in the woods, and how could the police get a search warrant to raid a sacred pine grove or a promontory known as Lunacy Hill?

The psychedelic yoga is the longest and toughest yoga of all, and the only way to keep it going is with a sense of humor. This has been known to seers and visionaries for thousands of years.

For me, the model of the turned-on, tuned-in, dropped-out man is James Joyce, the great psychedelic writer of this century. Pouring out a river-run of pun, jest, put-on, up-level, comic word acrobatics. The impact of Joyce via McLuhan on the psychedelic age cannot be overestimated.

Bill Burroughs is the Buster Keaton of the movement. He was Mr. Acid before LSD was invented. The soft-bodied answer to IBM. Unsmiling comedian genius.

Twenty years ago today Sergeant Pepper taught the band to play. The classic ontological vaudeville routine.

The Buddha smile.

The laughing fat Chinese sage.

The flute of Krishna tickling the cowgirls.

The dance of Shiva.

Om, the cosmic chuckle.

The sweaty belly guffaw of a Hasidic Jew.

Where are the laughing Christians? Something twisted grabbed the Christian mind around the third century. Is there any tender mirth left in the cult of the cross?

Mystics, prophets, holy men, are all laughers because the religious revelation is a rib-tickling amazement-insight that all human purposes, including your own, are solemn self-deceptions. You see through the game and laugh with God at the cosmic joke.

The holy man is the one who can pass on a part of the secret, express the joke, act out a fragment of the riddle.

To be a holy man, you have to be a funny man.

Take for example Lisa Lieberman, founder and chief boo-hoo of the Neo-Marxian Church. Authentic American anarchist, nonconformist, itinerant preacher. A pure-essence eccentric paranoid in the grand tradition of bullheaded, nutty women who stubbornly insist on being themselves and who are ready to fight at the drop of a cliché for the right of others to be themselves.

For five years this Lisa Lieberman has been a wandering guerrilla nun in the psychedelic underground.

When she first showed up at Millbrook in 1963, Lisa was a school psychologist, a big, blond, loud-voiced barroom intellectual. She roved around Castalia one weekend, grandiose, blustering, reverent, intelligent and too drunk to take LSD.

Then this oldest daughter of a Lutheran minister wrote a 1,000-page pilgrim's progress epic about her 3-day nontrip to Millbrook, running off 15 typed pages a day and coming back to Castalia weekends as Christian H. Christian, crawling painfully up the kitchen floor, splashing in the toilet bowls filled with whiskey, throwing out an endless monologue of corny psychological-psychedelic paranoia, and making feeble but mesmeric passes at Castalia's soft-eyed marijuana goddesses whom she hallucinated to be thirteen-year-old virgins. Like Dylan Thomas, so high, so juiced on her own cerebrospinal fluid, she accused us of slipping LSD into her food.

Then she got fired by her school board for some series of honest, rebellious, adolescent antics and, naturally, started her own religion.

WE MAINTAIN THE PSYCHEDELIC SUBSTANCES ARE COMMUNIST, THAT IS, DIVINE SUBSTANCES, NO MATTER WHO USES THEM, IN WHATEVER SPIRIT, WITH WHATEVER INTENTIONS. . . . WE DO NOT EMPLOY SET RITUALS, MAKE CONDITIONS FOR MEMBERSHIP OTHER THAN AGREEMENT WITH OUR PRINCIPLES, OR REGULATE THE FREQUENCY OR INTENSITY OF THE SACRAMENTAL EXPERIENCE. MANY OF OUR MEMBERS ARE DAMNED FOOLS AND MISERABLE SINNERS. MEMBERSHIP IN THE CHURCH IS NO GUARANTEE OF INTELLECTUALITY OR OF SPIRITUAL WISDOM; IT MAY EVEN BE POSSIBLE THAT ONE OR TWO OF OUR BOO-HOOS ARE OPPORTUNISTIC CHARLATANS, BUT WE ARE NOT DISMAYED BY THESE CONDITIONS; IT HAS NEVER BEEN OUR OBJECTIVE TO ADD ONE MORE SWOLLEN INSTITUTIONAL SUBSTITUTE FOR INDIVIDUAL VIRTUE TO THE ALREADY CROWDED LISTS.

Lisa Lieberman, the Martin Luther of the psychedelic movement, even when drunk, spraying blindly from her inkpot, the most courageous theologian of our time.

While the academics play word games about God's medical condition, Lisa, staggering insane in her study at three in the morning, tackles the real gut issues like: are marijuana and LSD really God's sacraments? Then, if yes they are, and Lisa says they are, then anyone who uses them, gives them, is involved in a divine transaction no matter how gamey, how nutty, how sordid his motives, so it doesn't matter who or when or how or why you turn on, it's still a holy cosmic process whether you are a silly thirteen-year-old popping a sugar cube on your boy-friend's motorcycle, or a theatrical agent giving pot to a girl to get her horny, or an alcoholic Catholic priest carrying the viaticum to a hypocritical sinner or even a psychiatrist giving LSD to an unsuspecting patient to do a scientific study. "It's all God's flesh," shouted Lisa, "no matter what your motives may be."

Oh, yes, let Lisa be given the credit. While the rest of us were still involved in research foundations and poetry conferences and trying to demonstrate that LSD was a nice, healthy, produc-tive medicine for virtuous, docile Americans, Lisa was roaring around in a turquoise convertible with a suspended driver's license, drinking bad wine from a bottle and shouting DON'T BOTHER TRYING TO CURRY FAVOR WITH THE ESTABLISHMENT—IT'S A LOSING GAME. WE AREN'T AMERICAN INDIANS WHO CAN BE PATRONIZED AND ISOLATED. CONGRATULATED ON OUR SOBRIETY, AND ALL THAT. WE HAVE THE RIGHT TO PRACTICE OUR RELIGION, EVEN IF WE ARE A BUNCH OF FILTHY, DRUNKEN BUMS. TRY NOT TO DEGRADE RIGHTS INTO MERE CLAIMS BASED ON EVIDENCE OF VIRTUE AND LACK OF VICE. WE DO NOT STAND BEFORE THE GOV-ERNMENT AS CHILDREN BEFORE A PARENT. THE GOVERNMENT STANDS BEFORE US AS THE CORRUPTOR OF OUR GOD-GIVEN HUMAN RIGHTS, AND UNTIL THE GOVERNMENT GETS ITS BLOODY, REEKING PAWS OFF OUR SACRED PSYCHEDELICS AND CEASES TO HARASS AND PERSECUTE OUR MEMBERS, UNTIL, INDEED, EVERY POOR WRETCH NOW SUFFERING IN PRISON BECAUSE HE PREFERRED THE MYSTICAL UPLIFT OF POT TO THE SLOBBERING ALCOHOLISM OF THE POLITI-CIANS IS SET FREE, OUR ATTITUDE MUST BE ONE OF UNCOMPROMIS-ING HOSTILITY.

Pageant magazine reporter: You call your local ministers boo-hoos. Why do you use such a ridiculous title?

Mona Lisa: We realize this title does have its absurd connotations, but we have intentionally chosen something with absurd qualities to remind ourselves not to take ourselves too seriously.

Pageant: You claim to be a church, but you don't take your own religion seriously. What do you take seriously?

Lisa: A lot of things. But one of the things we take least seriously is institutional life, the thing most people take more seriously than anything else. We think this is one of the faults of modern man: elevating institutional forms and structures to the level of eternal verities.

The wit and wisdom of this great psychedelic bovine is collected in a softcover book, *The Neo-Marxian Church Catechism and Handbook.* The Table of Contents reflects the flavor of this mad, disorganized masterpiece:

Pronouncements of the chief boo-hoo on:

LSD

MARIJUANA

SEX

REVOLUTIONARY POLITICS

Articles:

SYNCHRONICITY AND THE PLOT/PLOT

WITH LSD I SAW GOD

THE BOMBARDMENT AND ANNIHILATION OF THE PLANET SATURN

DIVINE TOAD SWEAT

THE REFORMATION OF THE NEW JERUSALEM

MORNING GLORY LODGE AND MILLBROOK

NEO-AMERICAN CHURCH GIVES 'EM HELL

THE 95 ITEM TEST OF NEO-PSYCHOPATHIC CHARACTER

FREE ADVERTISING AT GOVERNMENT EXPENSE

UP-TO-DATE LIST OF BOO-HOOS

CATALOG   CARTOONS

Readers of *The Neo-Marxian Church Catechism and Handbook* will learn that the seal of the church portrays a three-eyed, turned-on toad rampant over the motto "Victory Over Sexuality."

Tim Leary: "Lisa, I don't like your motto. It's a whiskey trip. It's not a psychedelic love message. Victory? Over? Sexuality?"

Lisa: "It's my trip. Take it or leave it."

You ask Lisa Lieberman what her goals are, and she tells you, "Money and power." To that silly end the last 20 pages of the catechism are designed as a Monkey Ward catalogue of items available from the Neo-Marxian Church, cash in advance, including for $30, a destruct box ("if opened improperly, contents go up in flames") and, for $100, a certificate stating that "the Chief Boo-Hoo never even heard of you and regards you with indifference."

Lisa's *Catechism and Handbook* is that rare commodity, an original, personal, unashamed, naked unveiling of a woman's mind, the Lisa Lieberman head trip. At times padded, at times so involutedly paranoid that you lose the thread, at times sloppily falling down, but always feminine, coarse, shouting, praying, and in touch with Central Broadcasting, the original, 2-billion-year-old Sunday night comedy show.

Lisa Lieberman came on the scene before the cool, gentle loveheads. She can't stand flowers. She hates rock 'n' roll. She has absolutely no sense of beauty. She is a clumsy manipulator, a blatant flatterer, a bully to the willingly weak, the world's most incompetent conman. She is, in short, a sodden disgrace to the movement.

Oh, pilgrim, if you come to visit the chief boo-hoo, you will see a sign on her door, "Parsonage, Neo-Marxian Church, Lisa Lieberman, Chief Boo-Hoo. Art for Art's Sake."

You ring the bell and await your spiritual teacher. The cover of the book flies open and there, reeking the fumes of a smoky, sweaty twenty-first-century Martian waterfront saloon, is the chief boo-hoo herself: glaring, wrinkled shirt, sloppy pants. Reading this book is a revelatory laugh-cry trip for those who are ready for it.

Last night Rosemary was lying by the campfire on a bed of pine needles, reading the *Catechism*. When she finished she looked up, her face beautiful in the red shadows, and said, "Lisa Lieberman is a funny woman." Rosemary is right. Lisa is a not-wholly holy, funny man.

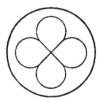

SEAL OF THE LEAGUE

9

*Homage to the Awe-full See-er**

At each beat
in the earth's rotating dance
there is born . . . "   "
a momentary cluster of molecules
possessing the transient ability to know-see-experience
    its own place in the evolutionary spiral.

Such an organism, such an event,
senses exactly where he is
in the billion-year-old ballet.

He is able to trace back
the history of the deoxyribonucleic wire
(of which he is both conductive element and current).
He can experience the next moment in all its meaning.
Million to the millionth meaning.
Exactly that.

Some divine see-ers are recognized for this unique capacity.
Those that are recognized
are called and killed by various names.
Most of them are not recognized;
they float through life
like a snowflake retina

---

* Reprinted from *Psychedelic Review*, No. 9, 1966.

kissing the earth
where they land in soft explosion.
No one ever hears them murmur
"Ah, there,"
at the moment of impact.
These men,
these "   's"
are aware of each other's existence
the way each particle in the hurtling nuclear trapeze
        is aware of other particles.

        They move too fast to give names to themselves
                or each other.

Such men can be described in no more precise and less
        foolish terms than the descriptive equations
        of nuclear physics.
They have no more or less meaning in the cultural games
        of life than electrons have in the game of
        chess.
They are present but cannot be perceived nor categorized.
They exist at a level
beyond that of the black and white squares
of the game board.

The "   "
process has no function, but can serve a function in our
        learning games.
It can be used to teach.
Like this.
Take an apple and slice it down the middle.
A thin red circle surrounds gleaming white meat
and there, toward the center, is a dark seed.
Look at the seed.
Its function is beyond any of your games, but you can use
        its properties.
You can use the seed.

The seed can teach you.
If you knew how to listen
the seed would hum you a seed song.
The divine incarnates, "   ," teach this way.
They teach like a snowflake caught in the hand teaches.
Once you speak the message, you have lost it.
Once you know the message, you no longer know it.
The seed becomes a dried pit.
The snowflake a film of water on your hand.

Wise incarnates are continually exploding in beautiful
        dance form.
Like the eye of a speckle fish looks at you unblinking,
dying in your hand.
Like cancer virus softly fragmenting
divine beauty in the grasp of your tissue.

Now and then "   " flower bursts in song,
in words,
"xywprhd,"
"P-8g @ cap,"
"evol."
The message is always the same
though the noise,
the scratched rhumba of inkmarks is always different.

The message is like Einstein's equation felt as orgasm.
The serpent unwinds up the spine and mushrooms
lotus sunflare in the skull.
If I tell you that the apple seed message hums the
        drone of a Hindu flute, will I stop the drone?
The secret of "   " is that it must always be secret.
Divine sage recognize,
message is lost.
Snowflake caught, pattern changed.
The trick of the divine incarnate can now be dimly
        understood.

He dances out the pattern without ever being recognized.
As soon as he is caught in the act, he melts in your hand.

(The message is then contained in the drop of water,
but this involves another chase for the infinite.)
The sign of "   " is change and anonymity.
As soon as you try to glorify,
sanctify,
worship,
admire,
deify,
an incarnate,
you have killed him.
                              Thus the Pharisees
were performing a merry-holy ballet.
All praise to them!
It is the Christians who kill Christ.
As soon as you invent a symbol,
give "   " a name,
you assassinate the process
to serve your own ends.
To speak the name of Buddha,
Christ,
Lao-tse,
(except, maybe as an ejaculation,
a sudden ecstatic breath like,
"Ooh!"
"Wow!"
"Whew!"
"Ha, ha, ha")
is to speak a dirty word,
to murder the living God,
fix him with your preservative,
razor him into microscope slides,
Sell him for profit in your biological supply house.

The incarnate has no function.
But his effect is to produce the ecstatic gasp.

Wow!
Whew!
God!
Jesus!
The uncontrollable visionary laugh.
Too much!
So what!
The stark stare of wonder.
Awful!
Awe-full!

SEAL OF THE LEAGUE

10

The Molecular Revolution*

Happy Thoughts

I am happy to be here tonight in what I feel to be a historic meeting of thoughtful and visionary people.

I am happy tonight because I just got word that my eighteen-year-old daughter Susan, who is in Laredo, Texas, today to be sentenced on a marijuana charge, received a suspended sentence and will not have to go to jail for 15 years. [*Applause*]

Salute to Allen Ginsberg

I have more reasons to be a happy man. It is good that Allen Ginsberg is here. Allen Ginsberg joined us at Harvard during the first two or three months of our research back in 1960 and along with Aldous Huxley can be considered as an early guru and architect of our work. He spent many hours sitting with us, telling us about what he had learned in Peru about how

---

* Transcript of a lecture delivered at an LSD conference sponsored by the University of California, June 1966. Because of hand-wringing on the part of university officials, the conference was moved from the Berkeley campus to an uncomfortable building in San Francisco operated by the University Extension. The small size of the hall limited attendance to 500 persons, about a third of whom were scholars, a third psychedelicists and a third police officers. Allen Ginsberg, who had accepted an invitation to the conference, was unceremoniously disinvited about a week before the opening on the grounds that "poets" have nothing to say about psychedelic drugs! Allen attended the conference, and almost every speaker opened his remarks with a tribute to the disinvited guest.

Curanderos ran yajé sessions. He told us about the drug scene in New York and in Berkeley and in Morocco. Allen is a walking encyclopedia of psychedelic lore. Above all, Allen taught us courage—taught us not to be afraid in facing those unknown realms of consciousness which are opened up by psychedelic drugs.

Beloved guru, I salute you. [*Applause*]

I am also happy that this conference was moved from the Berkeley campus to University Extension here in San Francisco. This is where it is, and this seems to be where it belongs.

University Extension and University Contraction

I would like to make a comment on the move, a piece of wisdom which comes from my cells. My cells tell me that at every level of energy there is a dialogue between structure and process, between free energy and the organization that contracts or controls the free flow of energy. It is necessary with every form of life and every level of energy to have to have this incessant dialogue of the surging outward, the extension, if you will, and the contraction, the control. Apparently this dialogue even exists at the level of the University of California, where we are led to believe that the opposite of University Extension is University Contraction.

The Department of Internal Chemistry

However, I respect both sides of this dialogue. Both contraction and expansion, both control and freedom are necessary. Without control we have chaos, void. Without expansion we have robot structure and death. If history teaches us anything, it teaches us that in every generation the surging energy of the new development, the thrust of the young idea, batters against the aging structure and then inevitably, within one or two generations, becomes part of the old static structure. Therefore, I predict that within one generation we will have across the bay in Berkeley a department of psychedelic studies. There will probably be a dean of LSD. When students come home for their vacation, Mother and Father will ask not, "What book are you reading?" but "Which molecules are you using to open up which Library of Congress inside your nervous system?" And the bureaucratic requirements will still be with us. You will have to pass Marijuana IA and IB to qualify for an introduction to LSD 101. Meanwhile, down on Telegraph Avenue, or over on North Beach, there will be the growing black market in RNA, and voices of alarm will be raised at the new chemical instruments for accelerating consciousness, enhancing memory, speeding up learning.

The same cycles repeat. Structure versus process. Young versus old. We are participating this week in a very ancient ritual.

The Old Movie—the Same Old Hopes, the Same Old Fears

For thousands of years, men and women have been meeting to do exactly what we are doing here in this room—to study consciousness. It's the oldest subject matter of all. How many levels of reality are there? How can we reach them? How can we go beyond symbols? In every tribe in human history there have been men who have specialized in these questions, and the entire tribe awaits their answers. There has always been this tension between the shaman and the war chief. I am sure that secret service agents of the Roman legions sneaked into the catacombs, waiting for the psychedelic services to start. The turn-on instruments, the cross and the chalice, were quite illegal in those days, you know. And later, Turkish Janissaries nervously watched the Sufi dervish dancers working out their elaborate and precise methods for getting high, for whirling beyond the mind through music and dance. And papal commissioners squirmed in Rome while Galileo turned them on in Florence with his telescope. It's one of the oldest games in history and sometimes I feel as though I am taking part in one of those old, old, late-night rerun movies. The same cast of characters, the same debate, the same fears, the same hopes.

But here we play out the drama in an awkward stage setting—

large hall made of metal. Spotlights and microphones. It would be easier and more orthodox if we were meeting in small groups on a hillside, or in a sacred grove someplace, because of the subject matter. It's a complicated procedure, this talking about the psychedelic experience to a psychedelic audience. There are many levels of consciousness, and actually, right at this moment, different members of this audience are vibrating at several of these levels.

Lecturing to a Straight Audience Is Simple

Now the typical, nonpsychedelic lecturer has to worry about only two levels of consciousness. His job is to hold the attention of the audience to the level of symbolic logic. He spins out one symbol after another. His main task is to stimulate. To keep the audience from falling into the two lowest levels of consciousness—stupor or sleep. The psychedelic lecturer faces a more awesome task. As I look around this lecture hall, I suspect that some of you are mildly stupefied by alcohol. If you have had two or three drinks before dinner, at some moment during my lecture, as I push symbols at you, one after another, your attention may start to waver and your eyelids flicker a little.

Many of you are stimulated by caffeine and ready to follow the sequence of symbols.

But I suspect that some of you here tonight are at a more expanded level of consciousness.

Compared to Lecturing to a Turned-on Audience

If any of you have smoked marijuana in the last 2 hours, you are listening not just to my symbols. Your sense organs have been intensified and enhanced, and you are also aware of the play of light, the tone of voice. You are aware of many sensory cues beyond the tidy sequence of subjects and predicates which I am laying out in the air. And there may even be some of you in the audience who decided that you'd put over your eyes that more powerful microscope and find out, "Well, where is this fellow at, anyway?" Perhaps you have taken LSD tonight, in which case my task is not to wake you up but rather *not to pull you down*. I have often had the experience in lecturing to psyche-delic audiences of having my eyes wander around the room and suddenly be fixed by two orbs, two deep, dark pools, and realize that I am looking into someone's genetic code, that I have to make sense not to a symbolic human mind, nor to a complicated series of sense organs, but I have to make sense to many evolu-tionary forms of life—an amoeba, a madman, a medieval saint.

Now another problem of communication tonight is that there are many professional and age groups present. We have just had a list of the many disciplines attending this conference, includ-ing the young and the nonprofessional. I would like to be able to speak directly and to make contact with every person repre-senting every social and professional group that is here tonight. That is my goal. But the problem is that you speak so many dialects.

I often feel in this situation like a United Nations interpreter trying to translate at many different levels the message I am trying to get across. You see, if I were to talk just to the young LSD users in the room, almost anything I chanted would probably get the message across. I could read the San Francisco telephone book and be greeted with enthusiastic applause.

Now, that's really not such a far-out idea. You see, the white section of the telephone book has a labeling and a space-time location of every ego game in San Francisco, and the yellow section has a listing, from Abbey Rents to Xerox, of every social game in San Francisco, and the turned-on person who listens to a simple recital of that gamut of game labels would get the entire evolutionary message.

So I'm not worried about the young and the turned-on. I am more concerned about the law-enforcement agents in this room, those whose job it is to turn us off. It is probable that there has never been a scientific, scholarly meeting in the history of our country which has had the benefit of so many law-enforcement officers present. Why are there so many secret police agents at these meetings? There is certainly no threat posed to property or person by the gentle people who comprise this audience. What is the threat that attracts the police? Perhaps it is the danger of new ideas. History teaches us that at other times and in other countries, police agents swarmed to meetings where ideas were discussed which challenged the power of the rulers. How does a discussion about the psychedelic experience threaten the power holders of this country? Is it because LSD and marijuana and the other psychedelic drugs may enhance individual freedom? Is our government afraid of internal freedom? I ask the police agents in this hall to listen to these lectures with an open mind. You may be learning about the future. You may even decide to join us.*

I Want to Talk About Two Things

First of all, I want to talk about the anatomy and pharmacology of consciousness. There are many levels of consciousness, and if we are going to make any sense of the LSD crisis or the drug controversy which is sweeping America today, we have to understand there are many levels of consciousness, many drugs which trigger off these levels and different social solutions for legalizing and controlling each of these chemicals. Second, I want to talk about the politics of ecstasy and to suggest a course of social action for these controversial times.

The Eerie Power of the Word "Drug"

We live, of course, in a drug-happy culture. There are very few Americans over the age of sixteen who don't use some dope to alter consciousness. Apparently we all agree that chemicals can change consciousness, but each of us tends to have his drug of choice to move to his favorite levels of consciousness. A tremendous breakdown in communication exists as soon as we use this

---

* At this point the lecturer waved merrily to two federal agents sitting in the third row, who smiled and waved back. Thus was affectionately celebrated the reunion with the two cops who busted the lecturer, his wife and his two children at Laredo, Texas, less than 30 months before.

word "drug." Drug! Drug! Now what is drug? It is a little four-letter phonetic burst—DRUG! Spelled backward, it is "gurd." It is one of the most powerful syllables in America today. For many people, for most people over the age of forty, the word "drug" means one of two things: doctor-disease. Drug-prescription-doctor-disease-medical control-doctor-disease. Or drug means dope-crime-dope fiend-drug-orgy-drug-crime. These are symbols, but they are powerful symbols, and I don't know how to change them.

Confident Youth and Fearful Age

Bernie Ganser, a reporter for Associated Press, told me a story today which depressed me. He said that on the plane coming out here, he decided to do a little consumer research survey. He asked the stewardess to ask the pilots and the other stewardesses and some of the passengers on the airplane what they thought of LSD and what questions they would like to be raised at a LSD conference of this sort. The pilot sent back the message, "How do you kick it?" The main concern of these middle-aged persons was how punitive should the laws be to control it. But to young people the word "drug" means something quite different. If you say "drug" to a young person, he says, "What kind? You mean alcohol that my parents lush up on every weekend? Do you mean heroin, that hang-up? Do you mean pep pills that I use before exams? Do you mean pot to make love?" The word "drug," of course, refers to an enormous range of human experience, from the Buddhist despair of the drug addict, from the hopelessness of the alcoholic, through a wide variety of positive terms—energy, fun, religious revelation, sexual enhancement, aesthetic kick, ecstasy, accelerated learning, and so forth. There is one factor in the formula to predict a person's reaction to LSD and marijuana. There is one variable which, if known, will predict better than anything else a person's reaction. It is age.

About 6 weeks ago I was on a Boston radio program. I talked for a while, and then people phoned in questions. The station censored the calls to a certain extent. They wanted to keep a balance of positive and negative questions. The first 10 callers were all positive. They were all young people, and they were asking serious, jolly questions about dosage, about oriental philosophy and psychology, about pharmacology, about scientific aspects of treatment and so on, except for one of these 10, who was an Indian philosopher from Boston University who said, "What the hell is going on in this country?" I couldn't answer that question.

But then, after a short break, the unfriendly and critical calls came. It was very obvious, the difference in ages. Tremendously concerned and deeply sincere quavering voices of the middle-aged and the elderly accused me of being a devil. A father of teen-age children said (in a heavy whiskey voice) that the station's license should be taken away. It was a rather eerie moment, and for the first time in the 6 years that I had been working with psychedelic drugs, I felt an animal sensation of fear running along my back at the anguish and the panic and the anger that was aroused in these aging minds.

The Eerie Power of Drugs

Now, why is there this fear, concern and hope centered on the word "drug"? I want to suggest some answers.

Consciousness is a biochemical process. The language of our nervous systems, the language of our sense organs, the language of our cells, the language of the genetic code, the language of memory, is chemical. We all instinctively know this. Somewhere deep in our DNA memory banks there is this intuitive knowledge that chemicals are powerful, that chemicals can change, that chemicals are the key. I think it's no accident that in so many myths passed down from generation to generation there is this theme of the magic potion. The myth is, of course, cellular wisdom. Symbols change, cultures rise and fall, but as long as human beings have had these kinds of bodies, living on a planet of this sort, certain myths keep appearing and reappearing. And many of them refer to the magic and wonder of the sacred drug.

At some point in the historic quest there comes the old crone with the potion. The old wizard with the elixir of life. Or it may be a frog or an animal or a witch with a cauldron or maybe a fruit or vegetable or a root or vine.

Corollary to this is the fact that control of chemicals which change the mind has always been a source of social tension. He who controls the mind-changing chemicals controls consciousness. He who controls the chemical can twist your mind, can alter your personality, can change you and your concept of the world. That's why there has always been this tension throughout history. The alchemist in his laboratory was a source of both wonder and fear. The man who can turn you on always stands there in the background of history. The aged kings of Europe sent their vessels out looking for that chemical. Ponce de León in Florida, seeking the elixir of life.

Everyone Wants to Control LSD

In our time the straight fact of the matter is that everyone wants to control LSD for his own purpose. The researchers will tell you, "Yes, LSD is a promising drug but clearly should be the property of investigators only." The physician will say, "Well, as a physician I will say that only the medical profession has the experience and responsibility to prescribe these chemicals for other people."

Then the religious people (and there are thousands of them who are involved in psychedelic drug research) tell you, "Well, there's no question that the psychedelic experience is basically a religious experience, but I'm concerned about all these youngsters taking it, because it's got to be given only by people with the most serious and religious motives in a place which is designed for the sacred experience."

Or the hippy looks at the scientists with amazement and says, "What are you trying to map and study and predict all this stuff for? Just turn on, man! Enjoy it!"

Of course, even the people who do not want to use LSD want to control it and want no one else to use it.

About two months ago I was in Washington testifying before a Senate committee. I was preceded on the stand by one Captain Trembly, who is head of the narcotics bureau of the Los Angeles Police Force. Captain Trembly is a good man and a sincere man, but he doesn't know what he is talking about. He is a classic example of the communication barrier between the generations. Let me give you three examples of the breakdown in communication.

Did You Say, Give LSD to Her Mother?

I came to Washington on this occasion with my two teen-age children. Captain Trembly told a story of a bizarre and danger-ous LSD experience that went something like this. "On February 18, our agents arrested seven teen-agers taking LSD. We took them to the station. One fifteen-year-old girl wished to go home in order to give LSD to her mother in her coffee cup so that they could reach a higher level of communication." MOTHER! DRUG! Senator Dodd looked agape at Senator Ken-nedy. "Did you say, 'Give a drug to her mother?' " Drug. Dope. Drug. Doctor. Disease. Drug. I looked over at my son and daughter, and we nodded. The person who has had a positive LSD experience naturally wants to share it with his loved ones. Of course this daughter wants to turn on her mother.

In Defense of Eating Bark off a Tree

Captain Trembly told a second story. He said his agents ar-rested two men on a lawn in Hollywood. They were eating grass and bark off a tree. Senator Dodd said, "Eating grass! Bark off a tree!" Captain Trembly said, "Yes, and one of them was a Princeton man." Well, I know that to any of you who have not taken LSD this sounds pretty bizarre. You think of these two men with a knife and fork and a plate dining on grass and bark. Actually, anyone who has been in communication with his cells realizes that from the standpoint of your DNA code this busi-ness of eating meat is really a fad that has just developed in the last few hundred generations, and that actually the DNA code in every cell in your body has been designing grass and bark eaters for about a million generations, that plastic steaks from Safeway still don't make sense to my cells. Very often during an LSD session a person does take a flower, take grass, take bark and reflectively chew it and relive the past. It looks bizarre, but it makes a lot of sense to your cells.

The Fuzz Holds the Drug

Captain Trembly then did a third thing which was extremely interesting. At one point he reached in his bag and he held out a bottle and he said, "This is LSD." Perhaps some of you saw the UPI wirephoto picture. As he did that, I was led to speculate. The facts of the matter are that Captain Trembly was the only man in the room who was legally allowed to do that. There were no doctors in the room with that special public health permit to give LSD in a mental hospital with a government grant. There was no one in the room with a legal right to stand there and hold that bottle. Senator Dodd could not do it. Even Senator Kennedy! Police power!

Anything which changes consciousness is a threat to the established order. This is one issue on which the entire spectrum of political opinions agrees. There's one place where you can get a John Bircher to vote side by side with a Communist. There's one place where right and left agree. Anything which expands consciousness is out! You have the strange phenomenon in California of both Governor Brown and Ronald Reagan rushing over each other to be the first to denounce our current key to the spiritual experience.

Chemicals Are the Keys to Changing Consciousness

Before you can understand or discuss the politics of ecstasy, you have to understand the anatomy and pharmacology of the different levels of consciousness. Consciousness is energy received and decoded by a structure. There are as many levels of consciousness in the human body as there are anatomical structures to receive and decode energy. Since consciousness is a biochemical process, chemicals are the keys to the different levels of consciousness.

This is the dizzying discovery of the psychedelic age. There are as many distinct levels of consciousness as there are neural, anatomical, cellular, subcellular structures within the human body. And chemicals to turn them on.

The mystical visionary experience no longer need be ineffable, undescribable. Consciousness (energy) is based on physical and physiological structure.*

The explosion of the psychedelic age is directly symmetrical with the multidimensional expansion of external science. Five hundred years ago man's perspective of the outside world was unidimensional—the macroscopic world of the naked eye, clearly visible or dimmed by fog or smoke. Then the invention of magnifying lenses brought into focus new levels of reality. Each new magnification structure required a new science, a new language to deal with the new level of reality (formerly invisible to the naked eye). Microscope, telescope, electron microscope, radio telescope.

Psychedelic chemicals perform exactly the same function for inner vision. Each class of drug focuses consciousness on a new level of energy. Each level of drug defines a new science and requires a new language.**

I have suggested in an earlier chapter that there are 7 broad levels of consciousness, each brought into focus by specific chemicals and each centered on structures within the body.

1. *Solar* (*soul*): Awareness of energy transactions among

---

* My equating consciousness with energy is based on my own psychedelic laboratory observations. I have been interested to note that in Tantric Buddhism and Tantric Hinduism the key term *vnam par ses pa* (or *vijnana*) can be translated "consciousness," "energy," "discrimination." Cf. Agehananda Bharati's profound text, *The Tantric Tradition*, pp. 84–85.

** It will be obvious to the alert reader that this is a restatement of the ancient Hermetic-alchemical formula—"What is without is within." Each level of energy which man has discovered outside exists within his body and is available to conscious discrimination.

molecular structures inside the cell—triggered off by large doses (300 gammas) of LSD.

2. *Cellular:* Awareness of energy transactions within the cell —triggered off by moderate doses of LSD, large doses of mescaline, peyote, psilocybin.

3. *Somatic:* Awareness of energy transactions within the neural plexes mediating organ systems—triggered off by moderate doses of mescaline, psilocybin, MOA, small doses of LSD, large doses of hashish.

4. *Sensory:* Awareness of energy transactions within endocrine systems and neural networks concerned with sense organs —triggered off by marijuana.

5. *Symbolic:* Awareness of energy transactions within the endocrine systems and cortical areas mediating conditioned learning—triggered off by seratonin, coffee, tea, nicotine, methamphetamines.

6. *Stupor:* Awareness of energy transactions within the endocrine systems and precortical CNS areas mediating affect and emotion—triggered off by alcohol.

7. *Silence-sleep:* Unconsciousness triggered off by chemicals (narcotics) which affect endocrine systems and precortical CNS areas mediating sleep and coma.

Seven new sciences of psychedelic psychology are thus defined:

1. Molecular psychology (psychophysics)
2. Cellular psychology (psychobiology)
3. Somatic psychology (psychophysiology)
4. Sensory psychology (sensory physiology)
5. Learning psychology (psychoengineering)
6. Emotional psychology (psychopolitics)
7. Psychology of the unconsciousness (psychoanesthesiology, psychoeschatology)

These levels of consciousness and the relationships between certain drugs and each level of consciousness are, of course, hypothetical. Psychedelic pharmacology and psychedelic neurology will refine and revise these speculations. The value of these hypotheses is that they are cast in operational, concrete, objective language. Take, for example, the statement: "Marijuana alters the biochemistry of the neural plexes mediating sense organs." This is a heuristic statement, i.e., it suggests a specific set of experiments. My language and my hypotheses are superior to the current language of psychopharmacology, which is bogged down in vague prescientific abstractions such as "Marijuana is an intoxicant" or "Cannabis is a euphoriant."

I don't care if my hypotheses are confirmed. I do care that pharmacologists and neurologists abandon their superstitions, moralistic language, and start studying the specific relationships between neural centers and different psychedelic drugs.

My task is not to be found "right" but to found the right sciences with appropriate linguistic sophistication to relate external events to systematically defined inner observations.

In the near future, each of these psychedelic sciences will be as complex and will involve as many scholars, technicians, educators as biology, physics, engineering.

Molecular psychology, studying the interactions between the nervous system and molecular events inside the body, will be as important as physics.

Each of these seven broad classes of inquiry will be divided into the obvious subclasses. Sensory psychology, for example, will include the following divisions:

psychedelic—optics
psychedelic—acoustics
psychedelic—tactics
psychedelic—olfaction
psychedelic—gustation
psychedelic—kinesthetics

Students will specialize in these fields. Enormous industries will be devoted to the production of the precisely formulated external energies which are required by the tutored sense organs of a turned-on populace.

In our present primitive state we have industries devoted to the production of the state of consciousness which I call level 6: emotional stupor. The liquor industry manufactures the chemicals and then sponsors the appropriate art form—TV shows which are perfectly tuned to emotional stupor. Aggressive, competitive athletic and political spectacles comprise the art form for the stuporous level of consciousness. The consumer is guaranteed a show of violence—heady sadistic victory for the winners, masochism for the losers, and another beer all around.

Is it, therefore, so far out to predict that in the near future a billion-dollar marijuana industry will sponsor art spectacles which will stimulate and coordinate with level 4—sensory awareness? The sensor-consumer will light up and then be entranced by mixed-media television art shows with erotic-meditative-Zen patterning designed for level 4 reception.

The cellular level of consciousness tapping the 2-billion-year-old pool of DNA memories will involve the most complex form of intellectual challenge and artistic involvement. You pop your level 2 pill, turn on your genetic memories, and take a specified reincarnation trip guided by a carefully worked out, multi-channel, multisensory, MV (multivision) show, sponsored, of course, by the Minnesota Mescaline Company.

Each level of consciousness will require its own art form. The 7 fine arts of the future will be:

1. Soletics—atomic-nuclear dramas
2. Genetics—evolutionary dramas
3. Som-aesthetics—bodily dramas
4. Aesthetics (erotics) —sensory dramas
5. Ascetics—intellectual dramas
6. Athletics (politics) —emotional dramas
7. Anesthetics—escape dramas

Psychedelic Science

During the next few hundred years the major activity of man will be scientific exploration of and education in the many new universes of awareness which have been opened up by psychedelic drugs. Man's inner fabric, his moist cellular terrain, his 2-billion-year-old unfolding pattern, is exactly as complex as the outer world.

Just as the instruments of external discovery have revolutionized society, so will the instruments of inner discovery.

Psychedelic Work

The key concept of the psychedelic revolution is work—ecstatic work. This central point is missed by enthusiastic acidheads as well as horrified burghers, each deluding the other with the notion of escape and naughty pleasure.

The ancient paradox remains. The more freedom, the more responsibility. The more energy released, the more structure is required.

Psychedelic drugs require much more discipline and know-how than turn-off drugs.

Narcotics are escape drugs. They require no disciplined training. Anyone can shoot up and nod out. Narcotics are blindfolds.

Alcohol requires little training. Very quickly each person learns what booze can do, where it can take him. Each person develops a crude emotional repertoire tied to his drinking. In any case, drink a quart of whiskey and you'll be flat on your back. There are 7 million alcoholics in the United States and 14 million more Americans who lurch through each evening in a heavy emotional stupor. Alcohol is like dark glasses.

Coffee, tea, nicotine, methamphetamine require no training for use. These drugs do provide more physical energy to play the conditioned chess game of reward and punishment. Heavy use of stimulants produces a jagged, irritable state of mild paranoia. The coffee-drinking, chain-smoking housewife paces the floor, twisting, twisting the black threads of her mental marionettes. "Speed" guns the heavy mental truck faster, faster down crowded highways to the next empty city.

The Discipline of Marijuana

Marijuana requires extensive training. You don't get the automatic chemical hit from grass. The marijuana high involves a subtle interplay between the turned-on sense organ and the external stimuli that bombard it. To learn how to use marijuana, you have to learn to use your sense organs. To listen to music behind grass, you have to log as much training time as would be required to understand and build a hi-fi audio system.

Few nonsmokers understand the sensory training necessary to groove with grass.

For the average adult, sense organs are game-playing cameras to pick up the cues of the game—red or black pieces on the checkerboard. The eye is clearly made to read the newspaper and the ear is clearly made to listen to the telephone. The atrophied sense of taste is connected with the fueling process of the robot. The body itself is a machine to move you through the sequence of chess game movements that make up your symbolic day.

The neurological fact of the matter is that the eye is a multilayered swamp of millions, hundreds of millions, of rods and cones, each one of which is equipped to receive light waves and to fire off an orgiastic belt when it gets hit by a light wave. You never see any "thing" or any object. From the standpoint of your retina there is just light bouncing off my face, off the microphone, off the blackboard. Light! Light, hurtling into the retina of your eye, the soft naked swamp of rods and cones, at the speed of 186,000 miles a second! Wow!

That's why artists enjoy using cannabis. Because they are not just seeing things. They are aware of and alert to this play of light. One of the first reactions to the psychedelic experience is, "Why, colors are so bright! The world seems alive! I'm seeing for the first time! It's alive! It's alive!" Well, of course it's alive! Your eye knew that all along. It's alive because it's nothing but pure light energy smashing into your retina. And those of you who have seen a psychedelic light show have some idea of what the psychedelic visual experience is. It's not just a sequence of tidy symbols one after another but an inundation, a Niagara of light energy.

There is no optical instrument that man will ever make that is so delicate and intricate as the retina of the eye. And the challenge is, can you learn how to use it? The same thing is true of the ear. The same thing is true of all the sense organs. The human body, as a matter of fact, is a collection of billions and billions of cameras, all ready to be focused, all ready to be turned on, to be harmonized and symphonized by the skillful user of this machine. I am convinced that very few people in the United States know how to use marijuana.

The use of the senses or the enhancement of the senses comes as a shock in our puritan American culture. We are a prudish people. It may surprise many Americans to learn that sensual training has for many thousands of years been a key spiritual technique in almost every religion in the world. If it sounds strange to you that the road to God comes through the senses, think about the Gothic cathedral. Consider the sequence of behavior that the medieval person went through when he walked in a Gothic cathedral, that glorious instrument for turning on. First he centered his eye on that rose window, a mandala. Then the incense began exploding like grenades in the olfactory bulbs in his nose with that one key message—it's not food, boy, it's not business, this is incense, the smell of God. The arrangement of the posture of the body, the mudra, the genuflection, or gesture of prayer, is a kinesthetic sign that you are centering your sensual energies to look within. The Gregorian chant, like the classic religious music of India and Persia, gets that drone going to remind you that this is a nongame process. That you are going within. If it seems surprising to you that marijuana can be considered as a key to the spiritual experience, don't forget that there are 200 million people in the world today who use marijuana regularly in their spiritual life or in their pursuit of serenity.

In terms of the optical metaphor, marijuana is the corrective lens which returns vision to sharp, clear focus.

The Discipline of Somatic Ecstasy

As one moves up the psychochemical continuum away from narcosis, more training is required. Thus the drugs which turn on the somatic level of consciousness (level 3) demand more psychedelic work than marijuana (level 4).

Hashish, MDA, moderate doses of mescaline and psilocybin

open awareness to messages from the autonomic nervous system, signals from the great organs and tissue centers within the body.

The average Westerner is aware only of the grossest emergency messages from within. Hunger! Pain! Suffocation! And Western psychology is equally ignorant of the long tradition of empirical investigations of psychedelic somatics by oriental psychologists. Tantric scholars (Hindu and Buddhist) have been describing and mapping somatic sensations for thousands of years. Elaborate and highly sophisticated manuals teach the science of somatic ecstasy. Tantrics call the centers of bodily consciousness *cakras*. The student is taught methods for turning on to this level of consciousness and systematic languages of color, sound, posture and symbol to communicate his observations.

Modern neurology confirms the psychedelic scientific explorations of the Tantrics. The brain, through the mediation of the autonomic nervous system, is in constant communication with somatic events. Your brain receives second-to-second teletype messages from your respiratory and circulatory systems. It is ironic that we seem to require the external probing of physicians to guess at diagnoses which are already coded by our own brains.

It is quite possible that within a decade, turned-on doctors will be giving level 3 psychedelics (like hashish) to patients, who will then be taught how to diagnose their own somatic ailments.

The Highest Kick Requires the Most Work

The sensory level of consciousness is limited to the few sense organs by means of which man makes his fumbling contact with the external world. The somatic level of consciousness is limited to the organs and tissue centers of the body.

The cellular level of consciousness puts man in touch with the DNA chain, which goes back to the origins of life. It is possible for man to tap into the unbroken wire of evolution, to decode fragments of the coiling blueprint. Most people who have taken large doses of mescaline or moderate amounts of LSD have clicked into the reincarnation line. The response to this experience is usually awed reverence, expressed in vague and corny religious mottoes. "We are all one!" "We are all leaves on the tree of life!"

Few hippies have understood the genetic implications of this experience and have realized that a new science of internal paleontology, ecstatic archaeology, has begun.

When I hear worried speculations about how man will use his leisure time in the automation age, I fail to alarm. The retracing of genetic memories back down through the myriad, multi-webbed fabric of RNA-DNA memories will be the major intel-lectual-ecstatic task of the future. The time will come within a century when an educated man will be he who knows who he is and where he comes from. Knows on the basis of direct psyche-delic experience.

The level 2 psychedelic chemicals are the microscopes of internal biology.

The use of level 1 drugs—LSD and STP—involves the knowl-edge of the advanced nuclear physicist. While almost everyone who ingests 500 gamma of LSD gets the solar vision, there is probably only one person in a thousand with the diligence and courage to understand and control the internal nuclear fission released by this miraculous chemical. LSD is the elecron micro-scope of psychology.

The "My God Is Better Than Your God" Game

One of the vexing social problems in the expansion and ex-ploration of consciousness is this: everyone has his favorite level of consciousness. One naturally locates God and all virtue in one's own favorite level of consciousness. The junkie does it at the level of complete void. The symbol-addictive person locates God and the meaning of everything in the center of his mental chessboard.

Many religions have been founded on revelations from the

sensory level of consciousness. Certain forms of Zen, the Hindu and Tibetan Tantra, early Christianity, frankly and studiously used the senses to find inner meaning and divinity. And most of these God seekers criticize, condemn, and imprison those who do not follow their favored turn-on method.

The classic Buddhist, of course, says frankly and straight off that he is not interested in the senses, that he is not interested in the symbol game, that he is not interested in the cellular transformations of the DNA code and that long, repetitious spinning out of bodies. He wants to get off the wheel of life. The goal of the Buddhist is the white light of the void, level 1, the silent prelife, preorganic off.

The "White Light of the Void" Game

One time we were running a training center in Mexico. That year we were using a Buddhist text, the *Tibetan Book of the Dead,* as our psychedelic map. The aim of the game was to move from stupor to symbol to sense to cell and finally to arrive at home base, the white light of the void. So we proceeded to do as human beings always do; we set up a hierarchical game. All sorts of invidious, competitive distinctions developed. "Well, I was in the white light 3 hours in my session last night." "Oh, you didn't make it at all?"

We are a species endowed and equipped with incredibly soft machinery which has taken the DNA code 2 billion years to develop, and we live on a planet with an enormous range of energies, light, sound, chemical, around us. The aim of human education, it seems to me, is to learn how to use all of these levels of consciousness, just as the person skilled in optics is able to shift focus from the dark glasses to the cellular microscope to the electron microscope, which reduces everything to a dancing mosaic of vibrations, and then slip on his corrective lenses to drive home.

Be very careful about locating good or God, right or wrong, legal or illegal, at your favorite level of consciousness.

The Politics of Ecstasy

This mention of good, right, and legal brings me to the final part of my essay, the politics of ecstasy.

To understand the current controversy over LSD and marijuana, I think you have to realize that we are right in the middle of that most amazing social phenomenon, a religious renaissance. The LSD experience is, and the marijuana experience can be, a deeply spiritual event. The LSD kick is a spiritual ecstasy. The LSD trip is a religious pilgrimage. The LSD gamble is that risk that men have faced for thousands of years if they wished to pursue what lay beyond their minds. The LSD psychosis is a religious confusion, an ontological confusion, a spiritual crisis. What is real? Who am I? Where do I belong? What's the real level of energy? Can I go back? Should I go back? Should I go on? How many of you can answer those questions?

When you hear about or read about a lurid account of an LSD psychosis, keep this hypothesis in mind. It may be pathology, but it might be divine madness.

Turn On, Tune In, Drop Out

My advice to people in America today is as follows: If you take the game of life seriously, if you take your nervous system seriously, if you take your sense organs seriously, if you take the energy process seriously, you must turn on, tune in and drop out.

Turning On

By "turn on" I mean get in touch, first of all, with your sense organs (not as instruments to be used in some secular game, but as cameras to put you in touch with the vibrant energies around you). Get in touch with your cellular wisdom. Get in touch

with the universe within. The only way out is in. And the way
to find the wisdom within is to turn on.

Now turning on is not an easy thing to do. In the first place,
it takes courage to go out beyond your mind. The psychedelic
yoga is the toughest, most demanding yoga of all. The easy
thing to do is to stay with your addiction, stay with the symbol
system you have. As you expand your symbol system from year
to year by building up a few conditioned reflexes, you learn a
few new words, a few new techniques each year. You will say,
"Well, I'm growing. I'm learning." But you are still caught in
symbols. The psychedelic road to divinity is neither a royal nor
an easy one. As I said earlier, to learn how to use your sense
organs with the help of marijuana is a very exacting discipline.
The discipline of LSD is without doubt the most complex and
demanding task that man on this planet has yet confronted. I
often tell college students, "If you want to get a Ph.D., count on
4 years after you graduate. If you want to get an M.D., count on
6 or 8 after your A.B. But for your LSD, count on 30 years at
least."

Tuning In

By "tune in" I mean harness your internal revelations to the
external world around you. I am not suggesting that we all find
a desert island and curl up under a palm tree and take LSD and
study our navels. As I look around at the people who have taken
LSD, far from being inactive, lazy and passive, I see them in
every walk of life and in every age group, struggling to express
what they are learning. The hippy movement, the psychedelic
style, involves a revolution in our concepts of art and creativity
which is occurring right before our eyes. The new music, the
new poetry, the new visual art, the new film.

Dropping Out

"Dropping out" is the toughest pill to swallow. Whenever I
give a lecture and tell people to drop out, invariably I alarm
many listeners, including my friends, who say, "Now listen,

Timothy, tone it down. You can't go around telling students to drop out of school, telling middle-class men with mortgage payments to drop out of their jobs. That's just too much! You can't do that in a technological society like this!" Of course, this message, *turn on, tune in and drop out,* just happens to be the oldest message around—the old refrain that has been passed on for thousands of years by every person who has studied the energy process and man's place in it. Find the wisdom within, hook it up in a new way, but above all, detach yourself. Unhook the ambitions and the symbolic drives and the mental connections which keep you addicted and tied to the immediate tribal game.

Is our American society so insecure that it cannot tolerate our young people taking a year or two off, growing beards, wandering around the country, fooling with new forms of consciousness? This is one of the oldest traditions in civilized society. Take a voyage! Take the adventure! Before you settle down to the tribal game, try out self-exile. Your coming back will be much enriched.

The Psychedelic Migration

Today we face a problem which is unique in man's history. Due to the population explosion, there is no place for people like us to go. During the summer of 1963 a group of us were deported from 3 countries to which we had gone to find a quiet place where we could teach ourselves and a small group of other people how to use our nervous systems. We made no demands on these countries. We actually brought money into these shaky economies, but we were barred. So as we looked around this planet, pored over maps and atlases that summer, it dawned on us that today, for the first time in human history, there was no place for people like us to go.

A hundred years ago, people who believed as we do in the spiritual life would get into covered wagons and move across the prairie. The Mormons did it. Or 300 years ago, people like us got into leaky boats and sailed for Plymouth Rock. And the fact of the matter is, there are many more people today who wish to follow a psychedelic way of life than there were Puritans in England who colonized this country. There are probably more in the city of San Francisco.

External migration as a way of finding a place where you can drop out and turn on and then tune in to the environment is no longer possible. The only place to go is in. And that's the fascinating thing about this new and indigenous religious movement which is springing up in this country today. It is interesting, too, that the psychedelic religious movement uses the same chemical aids or sacraments as the first American religion—the peyote religion of the native American Indians. I wonder if this is an accident or rather, perhaps, a curious game of the DNA code.

The characteristics of the psychedelic-spiritual quest are these: it's highly individual, highly personal. You will find no temples, you will find no organized dogmas; you will find instead small groups of people, usually centered on families, making these voyages together. We have discovered, as men have discovered for thousands of years, that the only temple is the human body and the place of worship is the shrine within your own home, prepared and lovingly designed for your spiritual procedure. The growth of LSD use in this country in the last few years is, if I dare say so, a minor miracle in itself. It has grown without any institutional backing or even recognition or approval. For the first 3 or 4 years it grew silently, person by person, cell by cell, husband and wife, you and your friends. My cells tell me that that's how everything durable grows. That's how it's always been.

When I say that the LSD movement is highly individual, I do not want you to think that I am talking about individuality in the personality sense. John Doe. Or Timothy Leary. I am saying rather that it's all located inside.

My Nervous System and Yours Is the Hinge of Evolution

From the genetic point of view, your nervous system and my nervous system is a hinge, a curious cellular hinge on which all of evolutionary history pivots. The cosmic Fox Movietone newsreel camera. Turn your nervous system on and focus it outside and you're tuning in on all sorts of messages and energy constellations that are out there, here and now. But if you focus your nervous system within, you will decode the cellular script and discover that the entire string of evolution on this planet is writ in protein molecules inside the nucleus of every cell in your body.

Be God and the Universe

Now here is the challenge. And it's the toughest and the most exciting challenge that I can think of. It is possible for you (in a way, you might say it is your duty) to recapitulate personally the entire evolutionary sequence. In other words, you can flash through the whole cycle yourself because the whole thing is buried inside your body.

Every generation lives the old drama out over and over again. Every person can. The challenge is for you to become your own priest. For you to become your own doctor. For you to become your own researcher on consciousness. Researcher. Now there's a tricky symbol. Research. The cop-out cliché is to say that research is needed in LSD. Who dares to say he is against research in LSD? Should LSD be turned over to the research scientists to study the implication and possibility of the experience? Nope. You cannot get off that easy. No government research project, no medically controlled scientific study, is going to solve your spiritual or emotional problems. And remember: the textbooks only tell you what you have to discover yourself. Have you ever personally experienced that the world is round and whirls around the sun? Please do not wait around in the hope that others will do it for you. The medical profession has had LSD for 23 years. And it has not come up with a use for it yet. And I do not blame the doctors. The psychedelic chemicals which expand consciousness are just not medical problems. LSD has nothing to do with disease or sickness.

When people talk about research on LSD, I have a little formula I go through in my mind. Talking about LSD is like talking about sex. Now I am not against research on LSD and I am not against research on sex. If some scientists want to hook people up and study the external manifestations of their internal experiences and if some people are willing to be hooked up and be studied by scientists during sexual or psychedelic moments, fine. But the psychedelic experience is an intimate, personal, and sacred one. And you, and you, and you, the individual man and woman, are the only one to do this research. And we cannot wait around, dealing with energies which are so insistent and important, until scientists or government agencies tell us that we can take that risk.

Drop Out into What?

Turn on, tune in and drop out. I want to be very clear about the term "drop out." I don't mean external dropping out. I certainly don't mean acts of rebellion or irresponsibility to any social situation you are involved in. But I urge any of you who are serious about life, who are serious about your nervous system or your spiritual future, to start right now planning how you can harmoniously, sequentially, lovingly and gracefully detach yourself from the social commitments to which you are addicted.

Well, what do you do after you drop out? This question was asked. A young man in the audience said, "Well, it's all right for you older, middle-aged fellows to go around lecturing on LSD, but what do we young people do?" There's so much you can do that it makes me dizzy to think about it. First of all, if you are serious about this business, you should find a spiritual teacher. Find someone that knows more about consciousness than you and study with him. And if he is a good teacher, he will teach you all he knows and tell you when he cannot teach you any more, and then maybe you can start teaching him or you will both go on your separate ways. But there's a tremendous amount of information which has been stored up for the last 3,000 or 4,000 years by men who have been making this voyage and who have left landmarks, guidebooks, footsteps in the sand, symbols and rituals which can be learned from and used.

Another thing you can do is to be careful with whom you spend your time. Every human interaction is an incredible confrontation of several levels of consciousness. The average civilized human confrontation is, "I bring my checkerboard to you, and you bring your chessboard to me, and we start moving pieces around. If we are cultured and civilized, I will let you make a few moves on your board, and then you will watch me play for a while. If we get very, very intimate and have a deep relationship, we might get to the point where I'll put some of my symbols on your board and you will put some of your symbols on my board."

Anyone you meet is automatically going to come on to you with a fierce symbol system. And tremendous neurological inertia takes over. There is a conditioned-reflex training which pulls you into the other person's game at the same time that you are pulling him into your game. The more I study the neurology of the psychedelic experience, the more awed and amazed I am at what we do with and to each other's nervous systems.

Only a Tiny Bit of You Is Policeman

Well, what happens if you drop out and leave school and leave your jobs? (And by the way, I address here not just the young people, but the researchers and the doctors and the police investigators here in the audience. You know, only a tiny bit of you is policeman, only a tiny bit of you is doctor.) If you want to drop out of your nonlove game and tune in to life and take some of these questions seriously, you do not have to go on welfare or go around with a begging bowl. The odd thing about our society today is that in the mad lemminglike rush to the urban, antilove power centers and the mad rush toward mechanical conformity, our fellow citizens are leaving tremendous gaps and gulfs which make economic bartering very simple. For the first thing, consider moving out of the city. You'll find ghost towns empty and deserted 3 or 4 hours from San Francisco where people can live in harmony with nature, using their sense organs as 2 billion years of evolution had trained them to.

To make a living these days for a psychedelic person is really quite easy. How? There's one thing that our mechanized society cannot do and that is, delight the senses. Machines can make things go faster and move more efficiently, but machine-made objects make no sense to your cells or your senses. Our country-men are fed up with plastic and starved for direct, natural sensory stimulation. As you begin to drop out, you will find yourself much less reliant on artifactual symbols. You will start throwing things out of your house. And you won't need as much mechanical money to buy as many mechanical objects. When you go home tonight, try a psychedelic exercise. Look around your living room and your study and dining room and ask yourself the question which might be asked by a man who lived 3,000 years ago, or a man from another planet: "What sort of a fellow is this who lives in a room like this?" Because the artifacts you surround yourself with are external representa-tions of your state of consciousness.

It's All Going to Work Out All Right

And now, a final word of good cheer, directed especially to those who are concerned about the psychedelic revolution. This revo-lution has just begun. For every turned-on person today I predict that there will be 2 or 3 next year. And I'm not at all embarrassed about making this prophecy because for the last 6 years Dr. Alpert and Dr. Metzner and I have been making predictions about the growth of the new race, and we have always been too conservative. Let no one be concerned about the growth and the use of psychedelic chemicals. Trust your young people. You gotta trust your young people. You had better trust your young people. Trust your creative minority. The fact of the matter is that those of us who use LSD wish society well. In our way we are doing what seems best and right to make this a peaceful and happy planet. Be very careful how you treat your creative minority, because if we are crushed, you will end up with a robot society. Trust your sense organs and your nervous system. Your divine body has been around a long, long time. Much longer than any of the social games you play. Trust the evolutionary process. It's all going to work out all right.

SEAL OF THE LEAGUE

11

Neurological Politics

Declaration of Evolution

When in the course of organic evolution it becomes obvious that a mutational process is inevitably dissolving the physical and neurological bonds which connect the members of one generation to the past and inevitably directing them to assume among the species of earth the separate and equal station to which the Laws of Nature and Nature's God entitle them, a decent concern for the harmony of species requires that the causes of the mutation should be declared.

We hold these truths to be self-evident:

—That all species are created different but equal;

—That they are endowed, each one, with certain inalienable rights;

—That among them are Freedom to Live, Freedom to Grow, and Freedom to pursue Happiness in their own style;

—That to protect these God-given rights, social structures naturally emerge, basing their authority on the principles of love of God and respect for all forms of life;

—That whenever any form of government becomes destructive of life, liberty, and harmony, it is the organic duty of the young members of that species to mutate, to drop out, to initiate a new social structure, laying its foundations on such principles and organizing its power in such form as seems likely

142

to produce the safety, happiness, and harmony of all sentient beings.

Genetic wisdom, indeed, suggests that social structures long established should not be discarded for frivolous reasons and transient causes. The ecstasy of mutation is equally balanced by the pain. Accordingly all experience shows that members of a species are more disposed to suffer, while evils are sufferable, rather than to discard the forms to which they are accustomed.

But when a long train of abuses and usurpations, all pursuing invariably the same destructive goals, threaten the very fabric of organic life and the serene harmony on the planet, it is the right, it is the organic duty to drop out of such morbid covenants and to evolve new loving social structures.

Such has been the patient sufferance of the freedom-loving peoples of this earth, and such is now the necessity which constrains us to form new systems of government.

The history of the white, menopausal, mendacious men now ruling the planet earth is a history of repeated violation of the harmonious laws of nature, all having the direct object of establishing a tyranny of the materialistic aging over the gentle, the peace-loving, the young, the colored. To prove this, let Facts be submitted to the judgment of generations to come.

—These old, white rulers have maintained a continuous war against other species of life, enslaving and destroying at whim fowl, fish, animals and spreading a lethal carpet of concrete and metal over the soft body of earth.

—They have maintained as well a continual state of war among themselves and against the colored races, the freedom-loving, the gentle, the young. Genocide is their habit.

—They have instituted artificial scarcities, denying peaceful folk the natural inheritance of earth's abundance and God's endowment.

—They have glorified material values and degraded the spiritual.

—They have claimed private, personal ownership of God's land, driving by force of arms the gentle from their passage on the earth.

—In their greed they have erected artificial immigration and customs barriers, preventing the free movement of people.

—In their lust for control they have set up systems of compulsory education to coerce the minds of the children and to destroy the wisdom and innocence of the playful young.

—In their lust for power they have controlled all means of communication to prevent the free flow of ideas and to block loving exchanges among the gentle.

—In their fear they have instituted great armies of secret police to spy upon the privacy of the pacific.

—In their anger they have coerced the peaceful young against their will to join their armies and to wage murderous wars against the young and gentle of other countries.

—In their greed they have made the manufacture and selling of weapons the basis of their economies.

—For profit they have polluted the air, the rivers, the seas.

—In their impotence they have glorified murder, violence, and unnatural sex in their mass media.

—In their aging greed they have set up an economic system which favors age over youth.

—They have in every way attempted to impose a robot uniformity and to crush variety, individuality, and independence of thought.

—In their greed, they have instituted political systems which perpetuate rule by the aging and force youth to choose between plastic conformity or despairing alienation.

—They have invaded privacy by illegal search, unwarranted arrest, and contemptuous harassment.

—They have enlisted an army of informers.

—In their greed they sponsor the consumption of deadly tars and sugars and employ cruel and unusual punishments for the possession of life-giving alkaloids and acids.

—They never admit a mistake. They unceasingly trumpet the virtue of greed and war. In their advertising and in their manipulation of information they make a fetish of blatant falsity and pious self-enhancement. Their obvious errors only stimulate them to greater error and noisier self-approval.

—They are bores.
—They hate beauty.
—They hate sex.
—They hate life.

We have warned them from time to time to their inequities and blindness. We have addressed every available appeal to their withered sense of righteousness. We have tried to make them laugh. We have prophesied in detail the terror they are perpetuating. But they have been deaf to the weeping of the poor, the anguish of the colored, the rocking mockery of the young, the warnings of their poets. Worshiping only force and money, they listen only to force and money. But we shall no longer talk in these grim tongues.

We must therefore acquiesce to genetic necessity, detach ourselves from their uncaring madness and hold them henceforth as we hold the rest of God's creatures—in harmony, life brothers, in their excess, menaces to life.

We, therefore, God-loving, peace-loving, life-loving, fun-loving men and women, appealing to the Supreme Judge of the Universe for the rectitude of our intentions, do, in the name and by the Authority of all sentient beings who seek gently to evolve on this planet, solemnly publish and declare that we are free and independent, and that we are absolved from all Allegiance to the United States Government and all governments controlled by the menopausal, and that grouping ourselves into tribes of like-minded fellows, we claim full power to live and move on the land, obtain sustenance with our own hands and minds in the style which seems sacred and holy to us, and to do all Acts and Things which independent Freemen and Freewomen may of right do without infringing on the same rights of other species and groups to do their own thing.

And for the support of this Declaration of Evolution with a firm reliance on the protection of Divine Providence, and serenely confident of the approval of generations to come, in whose name we speak, do we now mutually pledge to each other our Lives, our Fortunes, and our Sacred Honor.

The Constitution of Life

WE, THE FREEMEN AND FREEWOMEN OF THE PLANET TERRA, IN
ORDER TO FORM A MORE PERFECT UNION, REESTABLISH SPECIES
HARMONY, PROVIDE FOR THE PHYSICAL AND SPIRITUAL SUSTE-
NANCE, PROMOTE THE GENERAL WELFARE OF ALL LIVING FORMS,
INSURE A CLIMATE OF ECSTATIC PRAYER, AND SECURE THE BLESS-
INGS OF LIBERTY TO ALL CREATURES NOW LIVING AND THEIR
POSTERITY, DO ORDAIN AND ESTABLISH THIS CONSTITUTION FOR THE
UNITED TRIBES OF EARTH.

ARTICLE I: LAWS

Section 1: The Laws of God as expressed in the evolving
principles of Biology and Physics are the Only and Supreme
Power of the Planet.

Section 2: The governing of human affairs shall be based on
this basic principle: Love God and every living creature as
thyself. LOVE-EVOLVE.

Section 3: No rules shall be established by man which interfere with the harmonies and rhythms of nature or the rights
of other men or other species to evolve according to the Divine
Plan.

ARTICLE II: TRIBES

Section 1: The organization of Freemen and Freewomen into
small social units for the purpose of physical and spiritual
growth is recognized as a basic part of the unfolding Law of
Nature.

Section 2: Tribes are defined by territory collectively leased
from God and by an individual tribal style of life and worship
freely chosen.

Section 3: Tribes shall establish game rules governing their
own style of life and worship. Such rules shall have authority

only within the tribal territory and shall not interfere with the physical and spiritual growth of other species in their territory and other species and tribes outside their territory.

Section 4:   The territory and natural resources leased by any Tribe shall be proportional to the numbers of tribe members.

Section 5:   No tribe shall number more than 360 persons over the age of fourteen and under the age of fifty years.

Section 6:   While each tribe shall evolve its own style of self-government, the following seed principles shall not be violated:

a. No tribe shall manufacture or possess weapons (mechanical, electrical, or chemical) designed to maim flesh, cripple health, wage war against or coerce other sentient beings.

b. Police shall function as unarmed umpires to supervise tribal games and to isolate violence in emergencies. No person shall exercise police or judicial authority for more than three years.

c. No secret police. No secrets about other sentient beings.

d. Each tribe shall guarantee free and equal access to life-giving energies. Competition and artificial scarcities shall be allowed only in the case of nonessential things. Competitive and greed games shall be considered as therapeutic expressions of archaic impulses, throwbacks to earlier, prehistoric epochs.

e. The exercise of tribal authority—voting and rule making—shall be considered burdens assigned by God and the DNA code to the tribal seed bearers, those between the ages of fourteen and forty-nine years. Persons under the age of fourteen and over the age of forty-nine, in consonance with the obvious directives of the DNA code, shall be relieved of all secular obligations and be free to laugh, learn, play, love God and exist as Holy Children of the Divine Parents.

f. No tribe shall allow invasion or restriction of private behavior within the dwelling places, shrines, or bodies of Freemen and Freewomen.

g. No tribe shall compel or restrict the mode of education, free movement, or free communication within and between individuals and tribes.

ARTICLE III: ALL-LIFE COUNCIL

Section 1: Planetary affairs and interplanetary relations shall be governed by an ALL-LIFE COUNCIL. The ALL-LIFE COUNCIL shall protect the freedom of all species and individuals within the territories of the participant tribes and shall negotiate on behalf of Freemen and Freewomen with nontribal governments.

Section 2: The deliberations and legislations of the ALL-LIFE COUNCIL shall be binding on all tribes.

Section 3: The ALL-LIFE COUNCIL shall be composed of one representative, democratically elected, from each tribe. Tribal representatives can be organized into regional groupings. The deliberations and votings of the ALL-LIFE COUNCIL shall utilize all available technical means for enhancing communication and coordinating information.

Section 4: The ALL-LIFE COUNCIL shall also include representatives of every other species of life on the planet and representatives from future generations. These spokesmen for infrahuman and superhuman evolutionary forms shall be selected by the ALL-LIFE COUNCIL from among scientists who have exhibited concern for and knowledge of the needs of infrahuman and superhuman generations.

Section 5: The ALL-LIFE COUNCIL shall coordinate and harmonize the physical and spiritual growth of each tribe and species and shall not establish any law which favors the growth of any species or tribe at the expense of others. Human beings now living who do not belong to tribes of Freemen and Freewomen shall be considered and honored as belonging to a different species.

Section 6: A founding assembly of the ALL-LIFE COUNCIL shall be convened at the call of forty-nine tribes of Freemen and Freewomen who have maintained territorial harmony under a tribal constitution for a period of one year.

MAY THE WISDOM AND BLESSING OF THE DIVINE PARENTS GUIDE US.

Reader—Write Your Own

The inflexible, dogmatic teachings of our League for Spiritual Discovery (which naturally change every few weeks) hold that every human being is born divine and that the purpose of life is to rediscover your forgotten divinity.

Specifically, to relive, to regenerate, to reenact all the classic spiritual dramas in your own seed style and to add a few flourishes of your own to the good old double-helical fleshly prayer wheel.

Thus we suggest that anyone who takes the Divine Plan seriously will inevitably spend some time and energy attending to the ancient tasks.

Start Your Own Religion

(Sorry, baby, no one else can do it for you)

Write Your Own Bible

The Old Testament is exactly that. Old. The garbled trip diary of a goofy bunch of flipped-out visionaries. Don't you know that God's revelation comes to us today clearer and more directly than it did to Elijah, Abraham, Isaiah, Jeremiah? To deny this is to say that God and the DNA code haven't been busy perfecting the means of communication, the cellular receiving sets. Everything you ever write in your life ends up as your Bible. The record of your voyage.

Write Your Own Ten Commandments

The ethical dilemmas you face each day are similar to but different from those of Moses. His tortured hang-ups are not exactly yours.

Start Your Own Political System

On earth as it is in heaven.

The standard operating procedure for designing a life of ecstatic prayer and exultant gratitude is to write your own Declaration of Independence and constitute your own vision of the holy life.

You declare why and how you must drop out. The DNA code does it at every moment of moist, electric fusion. We were all conceived in orgasm.

The Declaration of Independence and the Constitution written by rebellious American colonists expressed, in 1776, some far-out notions. But there have been eight generations since then.

Today these two powerful documents are dangerously out of date. Dead parchment. You can't preserve Jefferson's seed under glass in the Library of Congress.

The Declaration and the Constitution reflect the vision of a mechanical, Newtonian clockwork universe. A static, Darwinian view of organic evolution. Survival of the fittest. Pick that cotton, black boy! A bullet in your head, Sitting Bull! The horrid assumption that the white Protestant human being is the center and measure of all things. Anthropocentric myopia. No planetary perspective.

The obsession with property, possessions, secular power.

Do you really want to live out the trip of bourgeois, slave-holding, puritanical Calvinists?

A basic exercise for the Freeman and the Freewoman is to declare and constitute your own righteous way.

On June 6, 1966 (the day on which the Sacrament LSD was declared illegal in the State of California), three young holy men in the city of St. Francis got high and declared their version of the vision: Ron Thelin, Michael Bowen, Allen Cohen.

A Prophecy of A Declaration of Independence

*When in the flow of human events it becomes necessary for the people to cease to recognize the obsolete social patterns which have isolated man from his consciousness and to create with the youthful energies of the world revolutionary communities of harmonious relations to which the two-billion-year-old life process entitles them, a decent respect to the opinions of mankind should declare the causes which impel them to this creation * We hold these experiences to be self-evident, that all is equal, that the creation endows us with certain inalienable rights, that among these are: the freedom of body, the pursuit of joy, and the expansion of consciousness * and that to secure these rights, we the citizens of the earth declare our love and compassion for all conflicting hate-carrying men and women of the world.*

We declare the identity of flesh and consciousness; all reason and law must respect and protect this holy identity.

This chapter presents another version of the *City of God*, written in those last days of the empire when assassination ruled the land and when gun-collecting huntsmen, themselves beneficiaries of the sharpshooters' aim, looked out the bulletproof windows of the executive mansions in Sacramento, California, and Montgomery, Alabama, and Washington, D.C., and denounced the gentle blacks, the graceful browns, the laughing students, the gentle longhairs.

Reader, write your own *Politics of Ecstasy*.

Printed in the USA
CPSIA information can be obtained
at www.ICGtesting.com
JSHW082211140824
68134JS00014B/557